BUYER BEWARE!

BUYER BEWARE!
CONFESSIONS OF A REAL LIFE 'ARTHUR DALEY'

Paul Nicholls

Published by:
Country Books
Courtyard Cottage, Little Longstone, Bakewell, Derbyshire DE45 1NN
Tel/Fax: 01629 640670
e-mail: dickrichardson@country-books.co.uk

ISBN 1 898941 76 9

© 2002 Paul Nicholls

The rights of Paul Nicholls as author of this work
has been asserted by him in accordance with the Copyright, Designs & Patents Act 1993

All rights reserved. No part of this publication may be reproduced, stored in a retrieval system, or transmitted in any form or by any means, electronic, mechanical, photocopying, recording or otherwise, without the prior permission of the author and publisher.

INTRODUCTION

The second-hand car trade has a very dubious reputation where honesty is concerned, bad enough at the more expensive end of the market, but at the cheapest end – bangers, anything goes; as the content of this book will soon make clear.

I may seem, after all these pages are read, to be some sort of un-desirable. Well be that as it may, but I can assure you, the reader – I am by no means unique.

The public at large are now safe in the knowledge that I am now 'retired'. One can only hope the discerning reader – yourself, learns a valuable lesson from this book.

Throughout this book, I have left out people's names or used a fictitious one to protect the innocent, or should I say – the GUILTY?

CHAPTER ONE

My *career* as such must have started some twenty years ago in the early eighties. Although for most of my working life I have been known, by people who claim to know me, as, 'a wide boy', a 'con-man', a 'shady character' and countless other less-flattering name tags. The fact of the matter is, my philosophy in life was, only put into life the minimum amount of effort required, but achieve the maximum possible result.

I did start life with conventional ambitions and expectations, unfortunately or fortunately, whichever way you look at it, my attitudes and outlooks on life were fashioned long before the age of eighteen, so my existence preying on 'Joe Public' was I suppose pre-ordained.

In my opinion a, 'con-man' is produced more by environmental pressure and outside influence which from an early age, other than by any amount of teaching or training alone, in other words we're born not made. I tend to go through life making comparisons, my observations give rise to some unconventional nick-names for individuals and types of people. For instance my belief is that in this world there are only two types of people, *Sheep* and more importantly *Shearers*. The sheep are the public or punters and the *Shearers* are the ones who take the wool from their backs. This is purely a personal view of course and can only be applied in a metaphoric sense. The art of making a living with the minimum amount of effort entails ensuring you're a *Shearer* and that your shears are very sharp.

My drop out, (from conventional career, mortgage, giving in to society's demands etc.) lifestyle was not my first choice by any means. When still a teenager I had more *normal* aims and hopes, indeed I stayed on at school to gain 8 C.S.E's and 2 R.S.A's when most fellow students decided to leave. I spent a couple of years in a promising career as a mine management apprentice. My future looked rosy. No one event altered the course of events, but over the years my awareness of *sheep* and *shearer* philosophy became apparent and you would not believe the abundance of *sheep* out there.

The trouble from a punter's point of view is that there are too many of you out there who still believe that your fellow man is basically honest, how wrong can you be.

The law protects the innocent members of the public or so we are led to believe, when up against a competent 'backstreet banger salesman' the protection of the law is akin to, being thrown into a cage with a wild bear and having a bunch of grapes to kill it with.

Basically, Trading Standards legislation relates to cars in two main aspects:

(I) Merchantable Quality – toothless when applied to bangers (only worries vendors of new cars.

(2) Roadworthy Condition – in short if the vehicle is safe to drive, all this means is, if the vehicle is up to M.O.T. standard and meets the criteria of the M.O.T test. The engine, transmission, back axle, interior etc, is not apertaining to the roadworthy condition of said vehicle. The aforementioned is then your bunch of grapes.

The classified advertising of cars is such that the average punter can find it very difficult to weed out the 'do up boys' from a genuine private seller. The problem being that if you are not a bona fide trader you do not have to advertise the fact that you are indeed selling cars on a regular basis to the unaware punter by stating it in your advert. Which means that he thinks you are a private seller. The good 'con' is going to keep up the pretence because 'Joe Public' is usually a very trusting animal, also the punter who thinks he is a little more streetwise believes that a better bargain is to be had buying from a private seller as opposed to a bona fide trader. I estimate that some 33% of cars advertised in small classified ads are in reality being advertised by someone hoping to make a profit. In other words not technically a private sale. Of course the majority of these are honest and trustworthy aren't they? After thirty years in cars and similar trading I can reliably inform you that in my opinion this is just not so.

The private seller is very hard to bring to book over any Trading Standards legislation. In fact it is nigh on impossible if dealing with the professional 'private man', as the author indeed was. To qualify my claim I shall digress a little.

In the mid-eighties I became a subject of interest to the local Trading Standards Department, due to a complaint relating to a car I had sold as a 'private man'.

The whole case hinged on a number of points but because of my 'education' I came out of the episode relatively unscathed and with a 'By Appointment to:' (well, in a sense, if you look at it with a wry sense of humour).

It all began with an unusually bad case of misjudgment on my part. I should never have landed myself with the car but I have never lost money on ANY car that has passed through my hands, and this was going to be no exception.

The vehicle in question was a Ford Capri 3 litre, some 14 years old at the time. The car owed me (the term means the total cost of the vehicle including any money spent on it) £175. It's main fault was that the engine was knackered, a very expensive item to replace on this model. Whilst cold the only indication of anything amiss was a tapping from the lower end of the engine. When warm the oil pressure gauge would drop to zero, a sign of a worn engine, to a knowledgeable person that is.

My strategy would be amongst other things, to firstly disguise the tapping – not so easy. To cure it properly would entail a complete rebuild, costing mega bucks = no profit – indeed, worse still, a great loss.

Now Ford V6 engines can be prone to other noises sometimes but these do not spell such dire consequences. e.g. noisy tappets, the cure is a relatively simple adjustment and yes, you've guessed it, this car suddenly developed a very bad case of badly adjusted tappets. The lower end tapping now 'cured', it only left me the problem of making sure whoever bought the car came when the vehicle had been stood for hours, i.e. cold.

The more cynical amongst you would say that as soon as the purchaser discovered a fault he would promptly return his defective purchase demanding his money back. Well yes he would. Putting aside the case in question for a moment. I shall explain my plan of action, normally it averts such an eventuality as this.

Whilst selling any banger the proficient *shearer* firstly builds in a few safeguards. I used to tailor my story and responses to suit each car I was selling, for instance.

Question, "Why are you selling the car? (as you make it sound such a bargain).

Answer, (This could take a number of forms). "Well I've just lost my job and can't afford to run it anymore" or maybe "Well I bought it to get me to a new job but it never materialised and I need the cash as I am deeply in debt, otherwise I would keep it because it's a great motor. To assist the aforementioned ploy one could add snippets like "well it's either the car going or the bailiffs". Depending on the gullibility of the punter – sometimes it doesn't pay to lay it on thick.

The above statements have (if you've analysed your victim correctly) created in the punters mind something along the lines. "well he seems a little over the top with the bailiffs but if he's skint I may get it cheaper."

Now the majority of banger buyers are looking for the unattainable, a brand new car for bugger all. So the nearer to this dream he can get the better he feels about the sale, therefore doing his ego a power of good.

The war of minds, (which I always win by the way) is almost run of the mill when buying and selling a cheap car. For every question the accomplished 'con-man' has a very plausible answer. To get back to the act of a punter trying to return a car for a refund, as previously stated he would not stand a 'cat in hell's' chance of getting his money back from a well prepared *shearer*.

Most complainants would first think out their case before

approaching the vendor.

My last word when closing the sale was to add the statement (whilst counting the victims money preferably) "Well it makes me sick because this lot (the money) will be gone in ten minutes time, but at least my debts will be a bit less now". Or something in the same style.

Any victim would therefore have this in his thoughts when working out what to do with his defective vehicle, also the fact that I am (to his knowledge) unemployed and so there would not be much hope of the *sheep* getting it's *fleece* back from a man of no means.

Usually the skill with which I had bodged the various faults on any particular car would mean the victim probably would not discover he had bought a lemon until quite some time had elapsed – another helpful factor.

Firstly your average *screamer* (as the complainer is termed by the car trade) might telephone to *rev* on you. The response would be one of complete innocence and surprise and great apology. "Well if I still had the money I would give it back to you, but as I explained to you when you bought the car I had to pay it out to settle some of my debts."

The punter, even if still irate, would probably give out the usual abuse and then hang up and seek further advice. His options are thus: either visit the local Citizen's Advice Bureau or if really annoyed a solicitor. The general response from either one of them first and foremost would be to advise them of their chances of gaining success from a man in such circumstances as I described, whilst quoting the saying used in legal circles relating to the purchase of second hand cars of:

BUYER BEWARE

Most less ardent *screamers* would more than likely chalk up the episode to experience by this time, especially as the sum involved (with the majority of the cars I sold) was usually less than £500.

Unfortunately for the punter concerned, this was not to be the case with the White Ford Capri 3 litre.

It all started with me placing the obligatory 'private advertisement' in the local press. Experience told me that to make a potential victim sit up and take notice is to ensure he turns up to look at your car first. Thirty years of selling revealed to me that on average, for every ten people that telephoned in response to an advert, only three turn up to view. Therefore the professional tries to increase this 'turn up' number by targeting his advert to the type of punter he wishes to attract. In other words accentuate the merits of the vehicle to appeal to the type of person likely to take an interest in that particular car.

In this example I was trying to 'pull' a 'poser', you know the type, young show off, out to impress, as the car in question, even with a knackered engine, had the beating of all the usual working-class posing machines, i.e. XR3i Escorts, Golf Gti's etc. This was a 'mans' car. Therefore I had to get the message across that their street 'cred' would be a lot higher than their mates if they were to buy this car. An added bonus in the attraction of selling to apprentice posers is the fact that, even though their conversation about cars seems knowledgeable, they are in my experience the most likely to buy a 'wrong un'. Young lads tend to buy what they see rather than worry about any defects, by 'young lads' I mean under the age of 25.

With all the former information in mind I placed an advert like so:

1973 Ford Capri 3000, 6 months tax, 11 months test, very good condition, only needs seeing, bring spare pair of underpants and £400 telephone ******

It had the effect of telling prospective buyers that it looked well and went really fast. The formula for any apprentice poser, and the potential purchaser would be the envy of his friends.

Low and behold my first prospect, after the old lying-through-my-teeth routine, screams down the road like a 'bat out of hell'. He was now £380 lighter in his wallet (I had knocked off £20, part of the strategy you know) about to become a member of the Alan Milton 'I've been conned by an expert' club.

Now, as previously described that would normally be the end of the matter, but this 23 year old poser thought he was going to teach me a lesson. Some of them never learn do they?

He had been gone about two hours after parting with his folding stuff when the statutory telephone call came, however this one had a

far from normal twist:
Screamer "Hello it's me, who bought your Capri."
My reply "Yes."
Screamer "Well my wife says I can't have it because it's too fast."
My reply "Well you told me that's why you wanted it in the first place <u>because</u> it's so Fast."
Screamer "Er yes but, has anybody else phoned for it?"
My reply "Well not yet, no."
Screamer "Well if they do, can you give them my number?"
My reply "Of course I can, I'd buy it back off you myself but I no longer have the money, as I explained when you bought it."
Screamer "Oh yes that's all O.K. as long as you can give them my number that'll be fine. Thanks."
(He's obviously a lamb and hasn't the courage to complain.) The *screamer* also thinks himself at this point, to be skilfull enough of getting the car 'up someone else'. There's one born every minute.

All this wheeling and dealing took place on Friday. I heard nothing from this particular punter all weekend. I did not pass on his number to any more callers, as quite frankly, there were none, what a shame. Monday morning arrived and so did the Capri, followed by his mate in an XR3i, the conversation went as follows :

Myself "Alright then mate?" (Always the friendly chap).
Screamer (Rather timidly). "Well not really this cars no good – it's had it."
Myself (With a smile). "Been thrashing it have you? Tut, tut."
Screamer (More assertively now – brave lad this). "No I F****ing haven't, and you know it. It was like that when you sold it to me."
Myself (With authority). "Look pal, you went over that car with a tooth comb before you bought it. You said you were a mechanic (they usually say that, young lads that is, probably because they think you'll be impressed by it, lambs to the slaughter). So if it was like that then, YOU must have known about it." (Evil bugger aren't I?)

Well the *shearer* I must remind you, the reader, never returns money and so:
Myself "Sorry mate you bought the car, it's yours."
I then closed the door and left the victim on the doorstep. He

promptly opened the letterbox and shouted "I'm going to the Trading Standards about this you bastard. You'll have to give me my money back then."

Off he goes with his poser pal in the XR3i, leaving the Capri parked two doors down from our house, unlocked with the keys in the ignition and the vehicles documents on the driver's seat. Any other part of Chesterfield an unlocked car, with the keys in the ignition, would probably have not attracted any attention, but well, yes you guessed it, the car was stolen the next day. OH DEAR!

The poor *screamer* thought that because he had left the car on my street it was now my property once more – how wrong can anyone get? The day of the disappearance he phoned me.

Screamer "Are you going to give me my money back? You'll have to sooner or later you know."

My reply "I'm sorry mate (sympathetic aren't I?) but even if I had got it I still wouldn't give it back."

Screamer "Well it would be better for you to give it me now or it will cost you more in the long run. (Very touching the way he's trying to save me extra expense isn't it?) "Sell the car again and then give me my money back then." (Public spirited this lad, I can sting someone else to get his money but I'm not supposed to sting him in the first place.)

At this time I did not know the car had been stolen, indeed, when the car was seen to be missing I thought he had collected the car himself.

Myself "Well since you've taken the car back why don't YOU sell it, as you were prepared to sell it on before?"

Screamer "Took it back, I've not took it you've still got it, haven't you?"

Myself "If you've not moved it then somebody's moved it for you pal because it's not here."

Screamer "Oh my god, I've got no car, and I'm down £380, you BASTARD." (Obviously a charm school graduate this one.)

Myself "Well I think you'd better report it stolen to the Police then squire, good day."

This so I thought was the end of the adventure, but no, silly lad was still hanging on in there, like a jaw-locked pit bull terrier. The sale of the Capri was in July. It was a freezing cold December morning whilst I was fixing the alternator on a Volvo, alternators for these cars are expensive items and the one on this particular car did not perform. In other words a fully charged battery went flat after a few miles running and the ignition light stayed lit all the time. The cure, step one, charge up the battery. The normal punter would be alerted to something being amiss when the engine was started if the ignition light didn't go out as normal. Simple disconnection of the warning light might be sufficient for most 'Do up' men, but the professional achieved a virtually undetectable bodge like so:

If a punter saw both the oil and ignition lights come on when the key was turned and then both go out when the engine started all would seem correct, whereas if the ignition warning light were simply disconnected a few may query it. The easiest way of doing the deception, is to remove the warning light wire at the alternator end, then attach it to the oil warning light wire in any handy well hidden place under the bonnet. This little trick saves the purchase of an expensive item of equipment and no loss of profit.

Back to the cold December morning. Two 'Gentlemen' approached with a gait normally monopolised by policemen on the beat. They were in fact officers representing the *shearers* toothless enemy – the local Trading Standards. After much discussion and my refusal to make a statement, away they went.

Nothing was heard from that quarter until January when a summons duly arrived listing the following charges:

1) Placing an advertisement likely to mislead i.e. stating the Capri was in very good condition, when it was not. The car had been recovered, although being stripped and burnt out, an engineer's report was obtained. He had found a worn track rod end and a section of the underside was quote 'badly corroded' contravening current Trading Standards regulations relating to roadworthy condition.

2) Being a motor dealer and not disclosing that I was trade in my advertisement.

3) Selling a car in an un-roadworthy condition, all supposing I

was a motor trader. These charges if proved, would mean that I was liable to a fine not exceeding £1000 per charge. Plus I would have to pay any costs incurred by the prosecution and also pay expenses of the *screamer* and compensation (£380).

The bulk of the prosecution's case lay with their ability to prove I was indeed a 'Motor Trader' whether officially or unofficially.

As for charge number 1) This, due largely to the evidence of the engineer's report, I could not really contest, I HAD called it 'very good condition' the evidence proved otherwise. A very good thing the car stolen was 'torched' as further examination i.e. the engine and other parts of the car, was not possible, how very fortunate. I had nothing to do with the theft of the vehicle as I subsequently assured the Police, when I was accused by them of the offence. Nevertheless it might have been a much stronger case against me if the car were more complete.

The second charge of not disclosing I was a motor trader, to corroborate their case, the prosecution, produced a number of photo copies of adverts in local papers over the previous year, all containing my telephone number. These numbered about 25, quick thinking and perusal showed that quite a few were duplicated, in other words the same car being advertised twice as it probably did not sell the first week and so got re-advertised. Yes unfortunately some cars you can't sell immediately, you have to select your prey for each vehicle, just in case some of you thought I was perfect and sold every car, first time, to the first punter, I'm not that conceited HONEST.

This left me with some fifteen or so cars to account for. Six I could put my hands up to, half a dozen cars in one year do not make a trader. The other nine I stated on oath (naughty boy I am) belonged to my friends and relatives who were using my phone as they themselves were not on the telephone. If the need arose, I said, they would all attend court and testify to that effect.

And so it was a charge that was dropped along with the third because I was not (and never have been your worship) a motor trader. The outcome of the case was that I received a conditional discharge for the first charge and ordered to pay £60 towards costs (which must have been quite considerable). As for the compensation, flattering the court and asking, that the *screamer* take up any claim regarding the vehicle, to the County Court, to avoid wasting their time with argument over actual in's and out's of claim or counter claim. The magistrates agreed with my request, meaning that should the victim try to get his money, he only had the protection of the far weaker County Court against me.

The aforementioned proceedings, was a long drawn out affair, about 18 months in all. I intended that any claim made by the punter would take equally as long in the County Court. This was of course to give him time to see the error of his ways and leave me, the poor *shearer* alone. Credit where credit's due the little tyke hung on in there through thick and thin, until the day of judgement arrived. After years of stalling the final saga was to be heard almost 3 years after the sale. Un-beknowing to the poor little *screamer* the law as it stands was not going to do him any good, and after my giving evidence and his silly Perry Mason impression, the judge summed up and gave his judgement as follows:

"It is quite obvious to me, that Mr Shepherd has been conned. Unfortunately for you Mr Shepherd, Mr Milton here, is a con-man who knows the law and apparently can use it to his advantage, therefore I must dismiss this case".

Whereupon the *screamer* said to the judge. "W-W-W-What does that mean." I got up to leave and whispered in his ear "that means Ian, you get F*** all, see you."

This case as I explained previously is typical (although I haven't discussed every detail of the case) of the vast majority of cases against the professional 'private man'. On a lighter note I suppose I could be called (as opposed to County Court judge and County Court Bailiff) a County Court Con-man, or for those with a weirder sense of humour 'By appointment to Chesterfield County Court'.

I would like to add a further observation to this case, in that to take a County Court action the plaintiff (the victim in this case) has to pay any expenses 'up front' hoping to regain them IF he wins the case. Although at the magistrate's court it cost me £60 it was well worth it to see his poor little face grimace in disbelief at the outcome of his case. It needs no great mathematician to work out that I was still in pocket on the deal. The irony of the whole affair is if he had not purchased the car from me, and had in fact gone to a bona fide dealer, he more than likely would have won his case. This is only one example of the phrase:

BUYER BEWARE.

Having shown the gullibility of 'Joe Public', I feel it only fair to demonstrate even bona fide car trade can be duped, not quite as easily, but nevertheless, a few have fallen prey, to this particular *Shearer*.

This specific incident took place some two months or so after the White Capri. The car in question, a Ford Escort RS 2000, was a wee bit out of my usual line, but a trader friend of mine was too scared to sell it, because of the state it was in, making it's faults too many to warrant any cash being spent on it. My fee for selling the said Escort was £200 to come out of the profit I made on it's disposal. Some may say the sale was somewhat risky, to a normal man anyway.

The car arrived on the morning prior to it's advertisement in the local paper. The advertised price was £1,650 the car owed my 'client' £800 and so somewhere in between these sums I had to find my 'fee' and hopefully profit for him. He had in fact 'got his leg in' with this vehicle (a term meaning that it looked likely you were going to lose money) and subsequently anything resembling his money back would have pleased him to say the least – in effect the car was only fit for spares and nothing else.

At first sight the Escort wasn't a bad looking thing, and it did possess a full year's M.O.T. (a dubious matter which I shall not at this time comment upon). The whole thing, even to my easily satisfied standards, was a definite candidate for 'Lemon of the Year'.

The old 'Blarney' was going to be on overtime on this one. The first pair of punters were the original time wasters, (lucky lads weren't they?) not even worth wasting my breath on. However the second caller just happened to be none other than a well-known local bodywork specialist, David Plum. Dealers sometimes descend on private advertisers hoping to land a complete Wally and 'pinch' the car off him. I was at an advantage he had never met me before. Normally one respects other members of the trade but, he took me for a mug punter and I was not going to inform him otherwise was I?

Well my story line this time was, "I'm selling it for my brother he's in the Navy and it's no good to him in there, so my Dad has told me to sell it for him". My wet behind the ears ploy is in full swing and he's swallowing it hook, line and sinker. The market price for an Escort RS 2000 was well in excess of £2,000 and the sly Mr Plum knew this full well, he's thinking 'I've got a real idiot here'. (From this point on I'm sharpening my shears.)

The car had of course been doctored to my usual first class standard. Although the body was quite sound, a number of other things were not so hale and hearty. The drivers door for instance when opened literally fell to the floor, due to the door pillar being, in short, virtually non-existent – cure – close the door after first cutting the linkage rods inside the door, rendering it un-openable once it was shut, therefore hiding the pillar from prying eyes. Excuse to the punter. "Oh I don't know why it won't open, it used to. I think the locks jammed." Plum is probably now thinking "God what a wally – looks like a minor job, a bit of penetrating oil and a screwdriver should do the trick. I'll tell this fool it will be an expensive job." This who's fooling who, carried on for quite a while. The list of bodges that I indeed did on the car would probably fill a book of their own. It took me almost a full day to do all the doctoring. I think I earned my 'fee'.

Mr Plum did of course find a few more faults, but the diagnosis he came to on each fault was the one I wanted him to come to. After all he thought his adversary was a mug not a master, so in retrospect he was the mug. Mr Plum had assessed the faults he had detected – even though he had only found 50% of them – as being minor in comparison to the profit he would make, so he thought. With the car 'fully' examined, and myself adequately assessed by him, as the run of the mill idiot who hadn't a clue what I was on about. (I should have got an Oscar for my performance.) Mr Plum came down to the nitty gritty and started to talk my favourite language, money.

After blinding me with what he thought was science, and telling me the truth, although he didn't know it at the time, it was going to cost a fortune to put right, he made me an offer of £1,300 (an insult of an offer even if the car was only as bad as he thought!) I duly said I would have to ring my 'Dad' to see whether or not he would accept his offer. (I had a funny feeling that 'Dad' would accept his offer.) I emerged from the house and informed Mr Plum that 'Dad' would reluctantly take his offer. He hurriedly counted out the folding stuff, whilst probably thinking at the same time, "About £50 spent on this, and that will mean a nice little earner of about £650, if I shove the car out at £2,000.

The car would have needed at least £1,000 spent on it to put it right, which made it somewhat of a White Elephant in anyone's book. A good day's work for me and £300 profit for my 'client'.

The following day I received a telephone call from Mr Plum. (Surprise, Surprise.) Threatening me with everything but castration and accusing me of telling "A pack of lies" and that the car was a 'shed' and if I didn't give him his money back he would do nasty things to my anatomy. (My he's a frightening man isn't he!) He also said he had made enquires and discovered that I was a trader and not a 'private man' as I had led him to believe.

I duly informed him that if he had indeed made enquires about me then those same enquires would tell him that he stood a better chance of getting feathers off a frog than getting his readies back from me. The conversation soon came to a swift end, when I threatened to make the whole deal common knowledge throughout the trade, thereby making him look an even bigger fool than he already was.

I did hear, from a scrap-dealer friend of mine, a week later, how he had just bought a smart looking Escort RS 2000 for breaking, and did I need any spares off the said vehicle. Needless to say I declined. I casually asked what he got it for and a sum of £200 was mentioned. I didn't ask the vendor's name, I just congratulated my friend on his purchase and thought to myself, "Another *sheep* successfully *sheared* poor Mr Plum."

The moral of this tale must be apparent to someone, I personally don't moralise at all, in fact I have been told on a number of occasions that I indeed have no morals at all. But no one can accuse me of prejudice as far as I know, in fact I'll fleece, anyone.

And now, as the saying goes: To something completely different.

One of my earliest memories of none car conning, began in the early eighties. It was to contribute very greatly to the career I have just turned my back on, (for the foreseeable future anyway, quite possibly for good).

It was during one of my many periods of, what actors call, resting, that this certain escapade sprang to life. A life-long friend of mine (yes a man like myself <u>does</u> have friends – the golden rule is that you never con a friend or neighbour, for obvious reasons, everybody else is fair game). 'Larry' Lamb, and myself were, as the saying goes, putting the world to rights, which was our permanent pastime in times of poverty. I can hear you saying, "If he conned so much how come he's talking of being broke?" Well, the answer is simple; although I have found it relatively easy to acquire the readies, I had a hell of a job (and still do) holding on to it once I've got it. I may be accused of being a lot of things, but being a miser is not one of them. When I've got it I spend it. I suppose the term 'easy come, easy go' was invented for me.

Back to the issue in question, Larry, was, and in my opinion, still is the best butcher around. (He'll be embarrassed now when he reads this book.) Not much of a claim to fame you may say, but teamed up with the best *shearer* I know, me, you have recipe for success, when aiming a con at the meat trade.

After a longer than normal spell of 'resting' our mutual search for a 'scam' resulted in the idea for the following chain of events:

Firstly we had to find a butchers shop. Then using his knowledge and acquaintances in the meat industry, coupled with my persuasive and convincing qualities, we could solve our current cash-flow problem – and what a problem, at a stroke.

Searching through the commercial estate agents we, quite by chance, discovered a likely business, (after a lot of reading between the lines and information analysis), which had recently ceased to trade. The vendor, after a long and searching telephone conversation, by 'yours truly', was, I deduced, skint. Not only skint but still having to pay rent on a shop no longer producing, or indeed capable of producing, an income. The position and state of the shop meant he was not going to find a buyer for the lease for quite some time, if at all. Prime territory for the enterprising con-man. We discussed our plan of action to the finest detail, I then arranged to meet the sucker at his shop with Larry in tow.

Larry and myself couldn't scrape up twenty pence between us. It was a Saturday afternoon and we were meeting the unsuspecting Mr Ridley, our unfortunate victim, at 2pm. We arrived a little after 2.10. (It doesn't pay to be to eager, it gives the impression that you are very interested in the place, therefore building up his hopes of a good deal in the offing. I wanted him fed up and in the frame of mind that any deal at all will do as long as his financial suffering ended. If he was lucky he could get his enquirer to take on the rent and pay him for the lease as well.) My first impression of our intended victim was certainly in keeping with my initial assessment, formed after our conversation earlier that day on the phone. He looked about twenty-five, as thin as a rake, (hardly the fitting stature for a successful butcher). He seemed shy, downcast, in fact the typical failure. I took an instant 'liking' to the wimp, if my assumptions were correct he didn't stand a chance.

It was patently obvious after ten minutes that things were going my way, it quickly became clear that he wanted rid of this 'business' quick-smart. After all, his shop was closed, he was deeply in debt because of it, and the ultimate insult was, he still had to pay rent every quarter whilst he was without a buyer.

He didn't tell me this of course, given the length of time the shop had been on the market, and analysing the information he gave me about himself it was easy to come to this conclusion. I only had to now work out how to prise the keys from his hand *that* day. The incentive being that in our inspection of the premises, we saw two chest freezers crammed full with meat. We could find a buyer within minutes for the contents, if only... Needless to say the old magic paid off and twenty minutes later Larry and I were walking down the road whistling 'We're in the money'.

All I had to do was offer him £50 a week and he melted. He was hoping for a lump sum of £1,500 but I convinced him to take us up on our offer by saying we'd give him £2,000, if he would accept it at £50 per week as well as paying the rental.

He accepted, because lets face it, £50 a week is better than nothing, plus I knew he had been trying to sell for at least 12 months, and that's a long time to get fed up in. We lifted a giant weight off off his shoulders the moment he handed over the keys, or so he thought. the mug.

It was now Saturday night, we had sold the contents of the freezers for £100 – a tidy sum in 1981, a lot better than twenty pence anyway. It would ensure we would not want for liquid refreshment and social life for the rest of the weekend at least.

Monday morning my task was to fill an empty shop with meat. We had all the fittings and fixtures, but any prospective customer might have used the witticism 'wot no meat'. Larry was the recent victim of redundancy. His job was, that of butchery manager with a recently closed supermarket. So he telephoned some of his ex-suppliers and managed to persuade one of them to deliver our first consignment of meat, on a week's credit, the next day. (A week's credit was the usual thing.) In the beginning, the first three weeks in fact, we did pretty well. We traded normally and made a living.

But making a living is for *sheep* not the *shearers*. Larry was, like most butchers I know, a gambler. He was therefore permanently skint.

We were solvent, we paid for the meat we were getting when it was due, and made a living. However this was not enough. We needed a plan to increase cash reserves. This was the outcome; I phoned a few more meat suppliers enquiring about credit, everyone seemed quite prepared to give it, but as they didn't know us quite understandably, they required a banker's reference or a trade reference. Our original supplier knew Larry through his dealings with them whilst working at the now defunct supermarket, and so they were prepared to take the risk.

Because we had been paying the original suppliers, Wilsons, I gave them as a trade reference, I explained as we were a new business – all the bank would say would be that we had only recently opened the account and therefore could not give an adequate reference. I had in fact not even opened a account at any bank. Indeed I have had a lifetimes aversion to banks.

Thinking that we were not going to be successful, we resigned ourselves to being legal butchers for a while, or at least until something else turned up.

Much to my surprise that same afternoon, I received not one, but two calls from new suppliers asking me to place an order – it had worked.

We were now, if only until we were caught, about to make a lot of money.

The ease with which we were able to get hundreds of pounds worth of meat virtually without challenge, was not, so much, the result of my stealth and cunning, but more a combination of the desire to sell, and the gullibility of the meat salesman, who is employed by a meat wholesaler. As the profit margin of these wholesalers is very small, in comparison to their actual turnover, it goes without saying that they rely on a large turnover of meat to make a living.

The fact that the salesmen they employ are paid commission on sales, make conditions ripe for the convincing con-man to fleece the supplier. Mr Average meat salesman is no match for a competent *shearer*. The trade reference we gave, we later discovered, was only checked upon (as was common practice). by the salesman calling them and asking; (a) if they had heard of us, and (b) did we pay up on time. Of course they gave the correct answer of, yes, probably adding that we, unlike normal customers in cash, was our way of settling up. Cash has always – in any form of deal carried it's own brand of respect, – unlike a cheque which could bounce.

This information in the head of a meat salesman could only aid our aims, after all, not many people would be as easy to sell to as Larry and myself. I'm all for making a man's job that little bit easier. (Considerate lads aren't we?) The crunch comes of course when we don't pay the bill. Then I'm afraid, the salesman's task in explaining to his employer, as to how we got away with so much meat on so little an acquaintance, is not quite so easy.

We initially placed orders of a small nature with both new suppliers. Wilsons, still got a small amount of business from us, after all we had to keep them sweet, they were to be our reference to obtain credit from any future new prospects. By the time I phoned the new suppliers for any fresh orders it was obvious that we would have to find a bulk buyer for the amount of meat we intended to order, as that amount would take too long to sell over the counter in the shop.

I found the outlet we needed in the form of a dishonest (but trustworthy enough not to ask to many questions) butcher called, shall we say Freddy? Now Freddy owned a small chain of family butcher's shops, and like everyone else we had cause to meet in this particular line, was very interested in meat at 20% below normal wholesale prices.

Freddy gave us his order, which was promptly relayed to our obliging suppliers, and we then sold it in turn, on delivery, to Freddy. It was sold as it happens at a loss, but what did we care? It wasn't our meat. The original week's credit was quite easily extended to two, and although reluctant, I managed to persuade them a further week. The day of reckoning however drew forever closer. We were of course both expecting a fair amount of screaming and aggravation when I informed the respective suppliers, that, we had gone 'bankrupt'.

Surprise is an under-statement. The suppliers were calm and collected, even sympathetic to our plight.

We simply asked if we could pay off the amount we owed (an impossible feat on dole money) weekly, explaining, pouring it on a bit thick, that it was due to our in-experience etc, that caused us to fail. We showed great willing to pay back what we owed, or so they thought. We offered them a paltry sum per week and they accepted with very little protest. I never realised how expert I was in the art of spinning a convincing story, until that day. We had got off virtually scot-free, with what amounted to, in the end, some £11,000 in meat at wholesale prices. I was fuming if I had known how easy it was going to be, conning the supplier, into feeling sorry for us when we went 'bankrupt', I'd have stung them for a damn sight more.

Some three months after we had gone 'bankrupt', we were sat at home skint again. Dare Larry and I try it again? Would the word have spread about us to other meat traders, thereby preventing us even trying? Could we find another shop? Did we in fact need another shop? All these questions and more were being discussed by Larry and myself, every night, well into the small hours.

Then, one night it was agreed that we should at least give it a try, but on a smaller scale. Pretending this time that we had got a shop, but we needed the meat pronto – not delivered, the next day, as was the norm. After all the 'scam' wouldn't have worked if they had to deliver to our premises, – a council house, not likely to impress a large meat company.

We still had one satisfied supplier though, Wilson's. Everything hinged on whether or not they had heard of the 'bankruptcy', when it happened.

As luck would have it they had not, they thought we were still trading and that we had just found a cheaper supplier, hence us not ordering from them for a while, or so they thought anyway. I gave them the excuse that our new supplier's quality had deteriorated somewhat and so we thought we would give them (Wilson's) another try as their quality was never in doubt. (What a smooth operator I am.) They swallowed it, and promptly took a small order from me – we couldn't afford a lot, we had to scrape up out of our dole money as it was for that. I stated that we were in a hurry as we had been let down by our current suppliers at the last minute. Therefore could we collect it and pay for it straight away. Yes of course we could. (You wouldn't believe the number of rush orders we had during the next few weeks, Honest.) Armed with our trade reference again we started, this time though keeping our order to each new supplier below £500 – "£200 each to myself and Larry after Freddy had paid us. This went on until we had run out of suppliers (around twenty in the north of England). We then of course gave each one of them in turn our 'bankrupt' routine, and offered payment weekly as per the last 'bankruptcy'. They all thought of course that they and Wilsons were our only suppliers. God forbid the outcome if ever they found that they were one of twenty.

After a few payments, in total about £20 per supplier, we stopped paying, as we had done a month previously to the original 'bankruptcy' victims. The gamble paid off, we estimated as in the first 'bankruptcy' that the sum we owed was a mere drop in the ocean compared to their weekly turnover. Given out present financial circumstances (unemployed), as they thought them to be, and without assets, it seemed a little fruitless to pursue the matter any further. It may have been a different affair had we not made any effort to pay the debts, or indeed if after offering did not make any effort to pay at all.

We did show willing at least even if through circumstances beyond our control we were prevented from keeping up the payments. (By heck I can sound convincing can't I?

The other side of the coin could well have been a long holiday, courtesy of H.M. Government. Our sheer bare-faced cheek and maybe the thought that most people in my experience think, that their fellow men are mostly good people (honest) helped us convince them, that our innocence and inexperience in business matters caused us to fail. Another school of thought might say we were very plausible liars and damn lucky to get away with it. The latter would have been my choice, had it not been for the fact, that not only had we been lucky once, not even twice, but numerous times. In point of fact, we didn't leave our efforts to just the North. The Midlands was our next hunting ground. With some quite comical events taking place.

I would have left the entire meat market alone for good, were it not for Larry and his addiction to gambling, and a small matter of me being broke at the time. (That makes a change doesn't it?)

A certain phrase came to light during this time, coined by Larry, not me. It led to me using it whenever his gambling got too much for me to endure, which was not an un-common event, although I freely admit we had a lot of laughs, due to his escapades arising from his involvement in the pastime. Whenever the unbearability stage was reached it was usually an early warning of Larry's intention to coax me into another 'scam'.

Maybe if I wasn't so easily persuaded each time his gambling might have been a little more restrained. But I consoled myself with the thought that at least with me to keep him in check, there was less chance of him coming a 'cropper' on a scam with me, than letting him fly off and attempt something on his own, probably with dire consequences. But he knew, that, although there was always a financial advantage to our ventures, I did them mainly, for the 'buzz' that I got out of pulling one over on the victims concerned. Needless to say his gambling got worse, the more he lost the more adamant he would be to win. I have never been tempted by the thrill of gambling. I suppose it's the belief that there is no such thing as being a lucky or unlucky person in my book. I believe, as the saying goes, that you create your own luck in this world, and that's the only luck I trust to.

Here we are again, both like a pair of greyhounds in the traps waiting for the hare to make an appearance, in other words, we were both of us skint and so woe be tide any meat wholesaler out there we hadn't yet *sheared*.

The, by now, statutory phone calls began, until we found a suitable mug ready to play ball. We couldn't travel too far as this may create an adverse reaction. (The prospect may ask himself, "why are they buying meat fifty miles from home, and wanting to collect it as well?) Therefore we limited our search for a victim to a twenty-five mile radius, it would then seem more plausible. Alerting our victim could lead to very serious consequences and I wasn't going on holiday for Larry's gambling or any 'buzz' I was likely to get.

I seem to have wandered again, sorry; We were talking of the phrase used to indicate Larry's eagerness to gamble. In a discussion one day I was sitting listening to Larry harp on about a problem he had got, (Financial of course, what else) when I happened to glance at the clock, it was 1.00pm – without much thought. I interrupted Larry in mid-flow, by saying "You'll have to be quick the first race has started." This prompted Larry, who was like all addictive gamblers, ashamed of his inability to control it, to say "The way you talk anybody would think I was 'bursting for a bet' all the tim Now gamblers will make up any excuse or indeed lie to cover up their gambling. I would liken the intensity with which Larry gambled, (he would always deny his addiction of course they all do, they could give it up today, if they wanted to couldn't they?), to that of a heroin addict. The fact of the matter is there are too many of both types of addict, but I am the last one qualified to moralise on either subject, and so therefore I shall continue; I'm afraid I did adopt the phrase 'boss-ting for a bet', as our north country accent portrays it, specifically to annoy Larry. I usually quoted the phrase when he was in the act of coaxing me into a 'scam' I didn't particularly fancy. It had the effect normally, of him, storming off in a huff.

But on this occasion saying "What's up Larry can't control the urge, are we, 'boss-ting for a bet again' didn't work. He was adamant that if I wasn't game for the third venture of conning meat, he would go it alone. Knowing full well he could not pull it off on his own, and the obvious desperation of his circumstances I reluctantly agreed to join him.

The victim duly analysed and approached, and after playing the 'trump card' (Wilson's), an order for £500 worth of meat on credit, to be collected that afternoon. This time it was Larry who telephoned, he was learning quite well the fine points of conning. He therefore became the 'boss' and in turn I the 'employee' in the victims eyes that is.

One problem stood in our way, no transport. An added drawback, the usual case, was we had no cash either to buy or even hire a van. Larry, I knew, had a closed current account, but was still in possession of the old cheque book. I said purely hypothetically, that if we could find a van for sale and give them a cheque, it being now Friday it wouldn't even reach the bank until next Tuesday by which time we would be in possession of our money from Freddy, a pity the account was closed. Larry informed me that the account wasn't actually closed, but that he hadn't used the account since being made redundant some six months earlier. He therefore assumed the bank had closed the account saying that he thought the account still open was going to be his excuse, he bit like a crocodile on my idea. An old Escort van priced at £150 was purchased with a cheque from a gormless youth who didn't even have a Bank account himself, but would see if his brother would cash it for him the next day. (This was too easy.)

The meat was collected, by me, pretending to be the driver for Larry's catering firm. That was a story duly worked out, that we were a catering firm supplying hotels and restaurants with meat. This was so devised because the catering trade i.e. hotels and restaurants, were known to be reluctant payers of their bills this would be a useful excuse, when we eventually became 'bankrupt'.

By tea-time the same day Larry had blown his share in the bookies and yes you've guessed it, was still 'boss-ting for a bet'. This in mind, he phoned the same supplier, of which I was completely unaware, requesting the same order for the next day, Saturday. Larry's obsession with gambling was seriously escalating. It looked like time for me to call it a day, as he got worse he was bound to make a mistake and spoil the whole 'scam'. I was in a 'Catch 22' situation. If I stopped now Larry could drop us both in it. I had to carry on, resigning myself to the fact that this was the last one. The next day I drew up to the suppliers for the second consignment of meat in twenty-four hours. Larry was waiting around the corner in a cafe picking his 'winners' for the day. Just as I was about to load up the boss of the firm approached and said "Has that boss of yours sent a cheque, because if he hasn't you're not taking any meat until he does." My God, a fine situation Larry had landed me in – obviously he hadn't learned as much as I thought. If he had, I wouldn't be faced with this problem. Snatching the phone from its resting place on the wall the boss said "Here you'd better ring him and tell him". What do I do now, I couldn't phone Larry could I? He was only around the corner." "He's not in the office this morning so I can't phone him yet mate." "Well you had better tell him to call me when you get back, I don't know him from Adam and this lot" pointing to the meat I was about to load up, "makes the total over £1,000 and I haven't seen a penny yet."

I assured him that I would pass on his message and drove off to give Larry the 'good' news. I parked up and went in the cafe and sat down with a cup of tea opposite Larry. He was too engrossed in the racing pages to notice me at first. When he did see me he said, "what have you sat down for, come on we've got to get moving." Such was the need for him to have the cash for a bet. I said four words "They've F****** us off." I then drank my tea before proceeding to tell him the tale. I thought "Ah a nice trip out, back home for dinner, then an amusing afternoon watching Larry swear and curse at the horses he would have backed, winning. When you don't bet on them, they always win, when you do, they lose. Sods Law. But this wasn't to be, such was Larry's need to gamble that day, he begged me to have another go. So we swiftly worked out a story for the supplier around the corner. Larry had to phone, letting enough time elapse to let them think he was in the office, from the call box outside. The plan went something like, "Mr ***** this order is for a new customer of mine and could lead to a very lucrative contract. I've arranged for him to pay me this first time in cash and so, (we knew his place closed at twelve on Saturdays) I could bring you the cash this afternoon, but please don't jeopardise this order etc, etc." It worked, due to the fact that it was now 11.30 and we had worked out, that if he let us have the meat it would not be left in the chiller until Monday – not as fresh by then, but more realistically, he probably wanted to bugger off home. With the promise of cash on Monday, by 12.15 we were driving off to Freddy's to collect our cash.

By the 3.35 race at Kempton that afternoon, he was broke. Not only broke, but hanging over him was, the cheque for the van, that would almost certainly book him a free holiday when it was discovered that, the account had not been used for sometime. Obtaining money or goods by deception would like as not, be the charge, and so there seemed no way out for Larry. It was up to me to come up with a plan to pull him out of the shit.

The fact that it was a weekend, and the vendor was no mastermind I hit upon the idea of returning to him with the van and saying something similar to this "look mate that cheque, we have just found out, won't clear." Better than telling him the truth that it would bounce sky high, "as his wages," pointing to Larry "have been late being paid into the bank by his employer. So I think the fairest thing to you would be for you to hold onto the van until Monday, and then I'll lend him the money to pay you, and then he," pointing to Larry again "can pay me back when his wages come through." The mug then replied, "Oh I see, alright then but what about the cheque then Quick as a flash I took the cheque from his greasy little hand, "Well if I keep this", with a smile on my face, "then I'll be sure of getting my money back from him won't I." Whereupon Larry dispenses him a false phone number. "Here's my number in case you need to get in touch with me before Monday, sorry about all this, it can't be helped but at least you'll have the money by Monday tea-time." We made a very hasty exit, leaving the gormless idiot thinking he's been frugal in holding on to the van until Monday. In my words, "so that you'll know he can't do you." He's still waiting.

Larry had learnt a valuable lesson, or so I thought. The usual apologies and excuses were performed to our latest supplier and our 'bankruptcy' went through relatively un-hindered, he squealed a lot, more than the others in fact, but he threatened the wrong things, County Court, bailiffs, etc. Obviously he thought the catering firm still existed, because he was sending bills to Larry for months before he gave up the ghost. Even if he had threatened us with the right people, the police, for his money, it was just mean we would have to sting one of his fellow wholesalers, to pay him that's all, no worries, as the Aussies say. I made up my mind though that I and the meat trade, from that day on, would part company – for good.

I always tread on the very edge of the line between legal and illegal, firstly because the pickings are much richer, and secondly to see how far I can go. I have learnt exactly how far one can go, without incurring the wrath of the law. Barefaced cheek with caution that has been my style. In fact if I were a cat-burglar I would probably wear two pairs of gloves – just in case. My approach may seem to some, devil-may-care and brazen, but there is no point, in my opinion, in inviting the law to 'come in and sit down' if you can't tell it to leave when you don't require it's company any longer. What I mean to say is, the weight of the law is fine when used to one's advantage, so long as you don't end up with the weight of that law, coming down on you. I am in fact expert in side-stepping and escaping it's impact.

Larry lasted two weeks before he came with the same old request of 'let's do it again.' Now as I have explained previously, l do most cons for, 'the buzz', but when the odds of the 'scam' paying off are not in your favour, you'd be a fool to attempt such a scam, and then of course you'd be like Larry. I refused point blank to try another coup, but even the old 'boss-ting for a bet' jibe wasn't going to put Larry off this time.

To cut a long story short, he went along and tried it on his own. He landed himself an eighteen months sentence at Sheffield Crown Court, they're famous for their free holidays.

Before his case came to court we did pull off another coup – not in the meat trade but in the world of 'greyhound racing'.

CHAPTER TWO

The following chapter is devoted to one of the most influential 'cons' I have, up to date, taken part in.

Larry was awaiting his court appearance (apparently cases heard at Crown Court at the time were taking some nine months to be heard). During this time he took an interest in greyhounds. I must add that, in fact, he had shown more than a passing interest, in them and the subsequent racing of them for a number of years. It just so happened that his interest turned into the yearning to be a greyhound owner. Well, it could have been worse – he might have set his sights even higher and wanted a racehorse. I suppose his motives were fuelled by the thought that being an owner might swing the odds a little more in his favour, or something along those lines.

Now before I go any further I shall inform the un-initiated amongst you, of the finer points of greyhound racing. In Great Britain there are two types. The first, and the one most people have experience of is that governed by the National Greyhound Racing Club, the N.G.R.C. for short. The second, less well-known is that of the non-licensed variety, known in the greyhound fraternity as 'Flapping'.

The former is very strictly controlled and can only take part at race tracks licensed and approved by the N.G.R.C., whereas the latter, not governed by the aforementioned but left to the individual, independently run race tracks themselves. It goes without saying that dogs in training on licensed tracks, and indeed the trainers of such dogs, are not permitted to race at 'flapping' tracks. The penalties imposed for any infringement of this rule are extreme, for owner, trainer and dog alike. Any offending dog or trainer could be barred from all licensed N.G.R.C. tracks for life. Any offending owner suffering the same fate. This being the case, any self-respecting trainer connected with racing on N.G.R.C. tracks therefore should never be seen in or near any 'Flapping' track.

Larry wanted a dog for 'Flapping', as N.G.R.C. racing could prove a very expensive hobby, what with the initial purchase of the dog, track fees, vet's fees, etc, before the dog even gets a race, let alone win. Not the type of greyhound racing Larry could afford.

'Flapping' could be a rewarding pursuit, if you had a fast enough dog, and only you knew its true capabilities.

For any greyhound to be allowed to compete at an independent track (apart from open races, which I shall cover later), it must firstly be 'graded' at a chosen track. Most tracks conduct this before the current races of that night are run, or on a non-race night, usually Sunday lunch times. The word 'grade' means in a word to qualify. Each track sets a minimum time for a dog to complete a set distance in order to 'grade'. If the dog is to slow it is not allowed to race at that particular track. This test is set in order that the track is not over-run with useless dogs. A second reason for the 'grading' process is to enable the person who makes up the race card (the handicapper) to place dogs of similar ability together and therefore make a fairer race of it. ie: a dog which is slower runs with low class dogs as opposed to ones of a better class, thereby making a race winner a foregone conclusion. The faster, better class would win every time) not much of a gambling prospect.

A dog's performance is recorded and the handicapper hopefully fills the race card with evenly matched dogs in each race. In an ideal world, there would be an even amount of good, fair, poor, very poor, etc dogs available to the handicapper. Because of the fact that different dog's, do in fact, run a race in different times, the handicapper compensates this by giving less able dogs a head start over the better dogs. The amount of head start is determined on the dog's previous form and times. The best dog in any particular race is run from what is termed 'scratch'. Slower dog's are then given varying head starts, depending on their past form. The handicapper in theory aims for what is termed a 'blanket finish'. A phrase meaning that at the end of the race on the finishing line, if a blanket was thrown onto the dogs, it would cover every runner. Needless to say this very rarely happens but it is a fair guide to the handicapper when trying to achieve a fair race.

Once your dog has 'graded' you are free to enter it in as many races as you wish at that particular track. The first race at the track, your dog will be handicapped using the time your dog achieved whilst 'grading'. Common sense says that if the dog only just managed to qualify, his first race should be with lower class dogs. All this information taken into consideration, the enterprising 'flapper' can increase his chances of winning if only he has a few, underhand, tricks up his proverbial sleeve.

For example, suppose the race track that you wish to race your dog at, has a 'grading' time for a distance of 500 yards set at 29.00 seconds. Let's say for the sake of argument that the fastest dogs at the track are able to run the 500 yards in about 28.20 seconds, you know your dog is capable of running the said distance in about 28.30. If you were to take your dog along and 'grade' it in at its probable time 28.30, the handicapper would duly place it, when entered for its first race at that track, in an event with the faster dogs. This would mean that the chance of your dog winning would be, if in a six dog race, in theory, one in six. Therefore the ideal situation would be that your dog be placed in a race with five lower class dogs. You could then be pretty sure of your dog winning. The chances of this happening are very remote you may say. Not so to the determined and enterprising owner. The answer is to ensure that your dog's full potential is not known until such time as you wish it to be. How do you do that? It's no good whispering in the dogs ear "Hey Fido hold back for a few races will you." But there are other ways.

In other words, when you 'grade' your dog in, slow him down, apart from running around the track with him still on the lead and you pulling him back to slow him down. There are two main ways to achieve a slower run from your dog.

1. Immediately before the dog is to run, secretly feed him his dinner before the race. If you have ever tried to run with a full stomach the result of this is obvious. The trouble with this form of 'stopping' your dog, is that any observant 'greyhound person' would see that he was full up and would therefore be wise, plus you cannot be sure that he could still run fast enough to 'grade'. (It may slow him down too much). At this point I will mention an episode concerning the slowing down method just described.

The two men involved in this little coup both had a dog each entered in a race and quite frankly, the other four runners were very low class animals and the bookies had made the two men's dogs first and second favourites respectively. The second favourite being a better prospect. (They would win more money if it finished first as opposed to the other dog.) They contrived to fix the outcome by feeding the other dog his dinner out in the car park prior to the race. As an added surety to the dog being full up and unable to run a good race. One of them went to a nearby fish and chip shop and came back with double cod and chips, which the dog eagerly ate as well. The favourite suitably 'knobbled', the two men placed all their money on the second favourite assured of a win. In the event the 'doctored' dog ran the race, leading all the way and winning by a very considerable distance. The pair were not only down a large sum of cash, but to say the least, somewhat puzzled as to how the dog they had so positively 'knobbled' had managed to thwart their so-called coup. The matter was soon clarified when one of the trap attendants was seen to be shovelling something out of one of the traps used in the previous race – a large quantity of sick. They had fed it that much trying to make certain that he lost the race, the overeating caused the dog to throw up in the trap and subsequently running the race of his life, making the bookies richer and his owners poorer as a result.

2. Is of course totally forbidden, on both N.G.R.C. and Independent tracks, and here again carries the risk, if caught of banishment for life. Indeed drug tests are regularly carried out

at licensed tracks. Although strictly forbidden, the practice is still carried on, (I personally believe on a much greater scale than some 'flapping' tracks will dare to admit).

Your second means of stopping your dog are –
Administer a drug in sufficient quantity to slow him down just enough to 'grade'. (The amount and particular drug is usually some form of human painkillers which determine the drowsiness of the dog, and therefore its ability to run a normal race.) There are always men in the greyhound world willing and able to supply these drugs and also advise you on the dosage.

Your dog if, 'slowed down' enough times, will eventually be placed with very low class dogs, it is then just a simple matter of letting your dog run a normal race, (After first placing a sizeable bet with the on-course bookies.) Barring accidents and acts of God, the dog wins and you go home a lot richer than you came.

With all the former fresh in his mind, Larry was hoping to buy a greyhound good enough to carry out a coup. He had one of his very rare wins, a princely sum of £200, and thought this sufficient to purchase himself a winning dog. I had my doubts. He had started to buy national publications aimed at the 'flapping' members of the greyhound world. In one particular issue, he found such a dog as he thought would fit the bill being advertised. The said dog was offered for sale by a vendor in Sussex. A fair run from Chesterfield. He asked me if I wanted to go with him, I declined as I thought a greyhound at that price unlikely to be of the calibre required to achieve any sort of success, but failed to convince Larry of the facts. He therefore sallied forth single handed on his futile mission. It was not long before my suspicions were confirmed. The vendors took Larry for some kind of mug, but thanks to my training over the years, he soon saw through their pathetic attempt at deceiving him, and came back, as he went, dogless.

His trip was not however a total failure, he told me of his conversation with the vendor's neighbour, a N.G.R.C. licensed trainer. The said trainer had a greyhound for sale, he (the dog), was a sprinter, as opposed to a long distance dog, which made him a 'flapping' prospect, as most of these races are over short distances, and his price, at first glance anyway, indicated he was a fast dog. His price for this flying machine, was £800, a substantial sum in those days. The vendor it transpired, was a prominent trainer on the South London greyhound track under N.G.R.C. control. For want of a better name I shall call him Shamus West.

Even though it is forbidden for trainers under N.G.R.C. control to 'flap' dogs, this does not mean the practice is not carried on. On the contrary the racing 'incognito' of dogs from licensed tracks by their trainers, in open races at independent tracks, is in my opinion quite a common occurrence, though hard to prove. All the trainer has to do is enter the dog, via a third party in an open race at a 'flapping' track. For open races, no grading is required and no real racing names are used, the dogs remain, like their trainers, completely anonymous if need be. This being so, if a trainer has in his kennel a very fast dog, he can, if he's prepared to take a calculated risk, make a nice little earner from the 'flapping' track bookies. Considering the fact that some dogs in training at licensed tracks may be worth thousands of pounds, therefore reflecting how good they are, the chances of them losing a race in a field made up of 'gifted amateurs' are very slim indeed. If the truth ever came to light, I think there would be quite a few red-faced trainers of top class dogs around.

Returning to Shamus, he had in fact gone one better than open racing at 'flappers' he had got a number of dogs in his kennel 'graded in' at a number of 'flapping' tracks throughout the south of England. He had never stepped foot inside a 'flapping' track himself of course, for fear of being recognised. The 'flapping' side of his kennel was undertaken by someone else on his behalf. The N.G.R.C. naturally was, and still is, completely unaware of this carry-on.

Shamus asked Larry if he knew of any prospective buyers for the said dog. If Larry is a fool with his money, he's certainly not stupid, and when asked this question by Shamus he immediately thought 'scam'.

Shamus gave Larry his business card. The very next day he was phoning the number on the card saying he had found a very interested party; me.

We worked out an 'identity' for me to assume. This turned out to be a second-hand electrical goods supplier, wishing to enter the world of 'flapping' with a half-decent dog. Now if Shamus was going to get me, Larry's punter interested in the dog, he would have to prove it's worth. What better way of proving the dog's ability than for him to be seen winning a race. This we presumed was the course of action Shamus would take in 'showing off' the dog in question.

This was not to be a difficult challenge for Shamus, if he was to follow the procedure described in the previous pages. Therefore we were assured the prospect of making a fair amount of money, by gambling on the said dog on the night of the 'showing off'. We also worked out and presumed that the odds on offer from the bookmakers at whichever track Shamus selected to pull off this coup, would be fairly substantial – as himself and some of his companions must also be planning to gamble on the dog.

Although we could estimate a lot of the events to take place at this display we could not know, the name of the dog, or the track at which it was to run. These facts to us were irrelevant, the salient point of the whole adventure was, as long as I fooled Shamus that I was genuinely interested, and capable of buying the dog, we stood to make a packet. We therefore had a number of problems at hand. The first being, the stake money – no need to bother with the whole charade – with no stake money. Although we had every confidence that the dog would win, we could not be sure what the starting price of the animal was likely to be. We had a rough idea that the odds were going to be greater than 2-1. After all to ensure the dog was going to win took time and effort, and so would hardly seem worth it, unless the rewards were going to be substantial, (2-1 or more).

The last and greatest problem of all was the fact that we didn't want to buy the dog – or at least I didn't. I was not going to give the greatest performance of my career to date, (On a par with Laurence Olivier any day), and only be paid for my pain and effort with a mangy mongrel, no matter how fast. In short I was doing all this for one thing, (well two if you count the buzz), the cash. Therefore it was agreed between the pair of us that we were to do this scam for the money alone.

Larry and I set off for London on the day of the race, having managed to scrape up a stake between us of £300 plus petrol money and a little for meals and drinks. We were to meet with Shamus outside the South London track where he was based.

It dawned on me straight away that this performance was going to be different from most. When Shamus drew up next to our battered old Datsun, in a Mercedes sports coupe, in those days a cool £40,000 of motor car. The car it turned out was driven by an owner-cum-friend of his, Michael Rourke, and not the property of Shamus himself. They in turn were followed by an old transit van, with his 'flapping' right-hand man and a kennel hand, as occupants guarding the contents of the van – two greyhounds.

Of the two dogs in the van only one, our prospective purchase, was due to run, the other came along, so Shamus said, as company for 'our' dog.

Shamus got into our car with Michael, and after the appropriate introductions and handshakes, instructed Larry who was driving, to follow the transit, leaving the Mercedes in the London track car park. I was later informed that this was so that when we arrived at the 'flapping' track he had chosen, we did not alert other local punters, to the fact that 'big money' was present at the track. This would only make the punters aware of a coup in the offing – as 'big money' was only there, usually for one reason. That was to walk away with even more 'big money'! If our intentions became known it could have any number of adverse implications, the most important of which was, that if it did become known it would alert the course bookies to the fact that a coup may be taking place sometime that night. This being so they would be very reluctant to take any large bets on outsiders thereby thwarting our chances of success. Therefore the flash car of Michael's was left in solitary confinement in the car park in London.

Shamus directed us to pull in at a pub car park after some forty-five minutes had elapsed. The transit carried on, and we saw by way of it's brake lights, that it to pulled up only some 100 yards or so further on and disappeared from our gaze. Shamus said, "The tracks just down the road, we may as well call in here for a drink, he's not due to run for another half hour." The track itself would have a bar of it's own, but for Shamus to be seen in there would have been a risk too great to take, and so the pub it was. Whilst in the pub, Shamus made me the subject of his attention whilst Michael and Larry attended to the liquid refreshments. He rambled on about pedigree, sires and dams, best times at this track and that, until the other two returned with four pints of golden liquid. Amidst great gulps of the stuff, the sandy-haired, short Irishman, struck me as a man who's total life from waking to sleeping had only one purpose, greyhounds. Now I pride myself on being able to sink a few pints along with the best of them, but this Irish human greyhound, amazingly, downed half a gallon of beer in thirty minutes. During this time, in fact the only time he lowered the glass from his lips, he continued to give me short bursts of his, for want of a better phrase, sales pitch.

We adjourned to the track leaving Shamus still in residence at the pub on his own. The race was about to begin and betting commenced with gusto, Michael started his and Shamus's punting from one end of the line of B bookies.

Larry and myself proffered our money to two bookies at the opposite end, I placed the £150 I had, on the dog at 4-1 and Larry did the exact same with the other half of the stake, placed with the bookie adjacent also offering 4-1. Both Larry and myself then shot off to the rails to watch the race, noticing that Michael placed a bet with at least four of the other bookies at the same price as we managed to secure. The dog duly won, of course our assumptions had been correct. Larry collected our £750 each and walked back to the car to await Michael's return. He was not far behind but did not seem pleased. It was a short drive to the pub, where Shamus was waiting – with a round of drinks. It was then that we were to find out the reason for Mr Rourk's dismay. He had in fact placed four separate bets of £400 each. He was irate because the fifth bookie along the line refused his bet at the very moment the traps opened, therefore, preventing him approaching another bookie in time to place another £400. He and Shamus had gone that night with the sole intention of staking £2,000 in total, on what was in fact an almost 100% certainty. He was annoyed at the fact that their total winnings were only £6,400 and not the £8,000 they had hoped for. Larry and I were over the moon with our somewhat paltry £1,200 profit – not quite a Mercedes Coupe, but enough. We did not of course tell Shamus that we had won such a sum, when asked we said that we had only staked the sum of £50 each, as we were a little unsure of the dog's ability, so we said, unlike Michael and himself.

Now I can sense that a few of you, are a little mystified. The fact you may say, that the dog was capable of being run to such an advantage, would make anyone want to keep a dog and repeat the coup, not to sell him. Not so, for one main reason, the dog was now a 'marked' animal, no self-respecting bookie was going to be caught with his pants down again, due to this dog. Therefore any future runs for the dog, stopped, or otherwise would see the odds become very short, thereby making a bet on the said dog not worthwhile, hence, now that his usefulness down South was over he was for sale.

After many more pints and talking we were close to Shamus asking me the dreaded question, the dog was now in the transit outside the pub, awaiting his fate. "Well Alan have you seen enough of the dog to make your mind up about buying him?" Came the question from a by now, half-drunk Shamus. I had by now, thought of a way around this problem and my answer was phrased like so. "Well Shamus I have been suitably impressed. He's a cracking dog, in fact just the dog I'm looking for. I'm in no doubt that I'll buy him off you, but I'd like to see him run on a tighter track with sharper bends, because the track I've in mind has a totally different set up to this one. Although £800 isn't a lot of money, (trying to sound the part at this stage), it's a lot if he can't run well enough on our tracks up North."

"Oh I can assure you Alan, the dogs 100% sound. He'll run to any hare or track," the by-now tipsy Shamus was saying. I kept him trying to reassure me going for quite a while. After half an hour of Shamus and I talking, Michael decided that he had to pick up his car, and so we all set off in convoy with the transit for Shamus's home ground. Leaving the vehicles, we all resumed our discussion in the bar of the licensed track. The discussion had a break for about forty-five minutes whilst Shamus went to the kennels to instruct his staff on the procedure to be carried out for tomorrow night's meeting – he had no runners this evening although racing was in progress as we spoke. It was during this break that Larry and myself struck up a conversation with Michael. I asked a question I later wished I hadn't. The conversation went something along these lines. "Well what's your line of business then Michael?. "Oh I'm a plasterer" came the reply in a soft Irish brogue. "It must pay well" interrupted Larry. "I've got a mate who does that, and he makes about £200 a week."

At this point I could sense that Larry was putting his foot in it again. Especially when Michael said, "Well I've got fifteen lads working for me at the moment, and they make about that, so I suppose you could say I make a bit myself."

Needless to say Larry didn't interrupt my act anymore that night. I struck up quite a conversation, and learnt a lot of things about Mr Rourke himself. The thing I found most interesting was the fact that, together with his brother Liam, he owned a racehorse and a steeple-chaser called, Erin's Pride,, (not it's real name of course).

It had only been raced the once and was due for a second outing the next day (Saturday). He said after being quizzed by myself, "He's worth a couple of bob on him tomorrow." Saying that would be all he would be putting on him anyway.

Well having seen the meaning of our Mr Rourk's couple of bob that very evening I thought it worth a discussion about the said horse with Larry later.

On Shamus's return he resumed his verbal assault to my ear-drums. I finally left him with the promise that I would phone him first thing in the morning, as I thought it better to find myself an adequate trainer for the dog, and had someone in mind, whom I couldn't contact until the morning. I said that I was 95% certain I was going to purchase the dog from him but I, being a man, liked everything and every aspect of a deal covered, before I commit my cash. I had to contact this particular trainer to assure myself first. He reluctantly accepted this, although I suspect he thought me some sort of 'wally'. This consequently saw myself and Larry, after saying our farewells, travelling North up the M I, £1,200 richer than we had journeyed down earlier that day.

On the return journey the conversation turned to the coming race tomorrow of Erin's Pride. All the night's events and the subsequent snippets of information analysed between us, it was decided that we should invest our evening's winnings on the much appraised Erin's Pride.

Without giving it a second thought we set about executing our planned race coup – part two. We divided the stake money up into £100 lots. We then had to distribute the said lots around the bookies in the immediate vicinity. The reason for our actions was simple, if the whole £1,500 was placed at just one bookie it may have affected the eventual starting price, as he would have 'laid-off' our bet by him placing the same bet with a bigger bookmaker. The reason for this being that if the horse did in fact win it could seriously damage his bank balance. (The 'laying off', of bets by smaller bookies is common practice, in short they can't afford to take the risk.) The fact of the matter is that sooner or later the consequent 'laying off' by all the subsequent bookies along the line could in the end affect the final starting price. Not many small bookies would accept such a large bet anyway. A hundred pounds placed at individual betting offices would therefore, not arouse much suspicion.

To our surprise in the event, the race in which our horse 'Erin's Pride' was to run, ante-post betting odds were being offered, and so we took the price, at each bookies in turn, of 7-2, thereby ensuring if the betting was brisk we would not be 'out of pocket'.

In Larry's words, "You know what these Paddies are like, they all bet, and when the word gets out they'll all be backing it, and we'll be lucky if the starting price is 2-1." By taking the price of 7-2 we were, if Erin's Pride won, going to turn an initial investment of £300 into £6,750 in less than twenty-four hours. Not a bad little earner.

The race started at 3.05, the distance, two miles, the racecourse, Newbury, and we were perched in Ladbrokes on two stools, listening to the commentary. Our horse was in the front five most of the way and 'riding handy' or so the terminology goes. The race is in the bag, it only had to run the final 300 yards to win by a fair distance. We were counting the money. The commentary went like this. "Erin's Pride is over the last and four lengths clear of the rest of the field, he strides up towards the line now, but making ground now is 'The Mill' and closing very fast on the leader now, they are stride for stride as they approach the line, they've gone past together, it's a photograph." Larry and myself were speechless, we dare not say a word for fear of missing the result of the photograph being announced. The loudspeaker sprang to life, "The result of the photograph at Newbury is; first number twelve The Mill, and second, number four Erin's Pride." We didn't hear the rest and we still didn't speak.

A look at the race card revealed that The Mill had never raced before and to this present day has never run again since. Someone, obviously, was pulling a coup of their own that day. The Mill had a starting price of 16-1. The irony of the whole affair is that, Erin's Pride ran his next eight races and won. Needless to say I never had a bet on him in any of those races. I must add that my gambling career came to a swift end that fateful day.

Some would say that Shamus West was avenged that day, who knows perhaps Michael Rourke fed us a bad tip that night, purely because I didn't buy Shamus's dog, I think not. If there is a moral in this particular story, for the moment it escapes me, as did the £6,750 that Larry and I expected to receive.

The whole episode gives rise to the old saying of, in racing there is only one winner – the bookies. This maybe so – I could say, "Ah but only if..."

Maybe I should not have written the previous pages, as they tend to expel the myth I have created of the *sheep* and the *shearer*. In the aforementioned case it gives the impression that I am in fact the *sheep* in this particular instance. This being so, I soon grew my fleece again, with the assistance of 'Joe Public' of course. I tend to look upon the experience more in the line of a lesson learnt. After all, every good craftsman has to be taught his craft to begin with, it just so happens that my training is gained from self-experience. There is as yet no known correct way of learning the art of 'conning'. Your degree of success on this voyage depends on the risks one takes and whether or not you survive the outcome. Nothing ventured, nothing gained, is a philosophy I try to live by. But to do this and stay within the confines of the law, becomes an ever increasing task. Once life becomes a little too boring, it was watch out there's a 'scam' about.

The last few lines can possibly be illustrated by a little expedition

I can describe as illuminating, and a valuable addition to my career; if you believe that you'll believe anything, read on. It's amusing if nothing else.

A week after the failed coup with Erin's Pride, Larry came around, with a, in his words not mine, 'cracking idea'. He was clutching a copy of, 'The Meat Trades Journal' a publication aimed at all branches of the meat trade, Larry used to buy it on 'dole money day'. The only day he was guaranteed to have any cash, at least until the first race started anyway. His exact terminology escapes me for the minute, but his attitude was one of 'this one will work'. I was not so sure.

Now I know I have said previously that I had retired from the meat trade, but this current idea of Larry's captured my interest. He pointed to an advertisement offering knacker meat for sale at the princely sum of ten pence a pound. Knacker meat as you probably will know is <u>not</u> for human consumption. The only outward difference between knacker meat and ordinary meat, is the presence of a purple-blue dye on the outside of the carcass. This is for the obvious purpose of making the meat instantly recognisable. Larry assured me that this dye was, if sprayed on, the usual case for a one man outfit, (most knacker men are one man outfits) easily trimmed off. This done the meat looks just as 'normal' meat does.

I was very dubious about the information that Larry had imparted to me, but always the eternal optimist I craved more proof of his statement. After all, meat at ten pence a pound which could be offloaded to Freddy at fifty pence a pound, was always worth a closer inspection. Still dubious, especially with Larry's list of successes to date, fresh in my mind. I told Larry to come up with something more concrete, and then I might be interested. It was not long before he came back, he had telephoned the number in the advertisement, gaining directions to the place in question.

Asking me to go with him was his next move. I had meanwhile, unknown to Larry, made enquiries about the purchase and sale of such meat. Apparently, to buy for resale, any knacker meat would require a license, and the granting of such a license was subject to very stringent conditions. This I confronted Larry with, saying that in such circumstances, no self-respecting knacker man would sell us any meat. But Larry was way ahead of me in this particular instance. He said that he had phoned posing as a private punter wanting meat for his greyhounds. After such deliberation I thought, what the hell I'm sat here skint, it won't hurt to go along for the ride.

The 'ride' it turned out, was to be to a place in the middle of nowhere, a small village in the south of England, curiously named Cowfold. If the distance was not to be off-putting, the vehicle in which we were to endure the journey certainly was. The vehicle in question was borrowed from one of Larry's gambling mates – it was an extremely battered old Hillman Avenger. The most memorable thing about this car was it's door fastening method. The door catches were not functioning properly and the method of securing them was by a rope stretched between the opposite doors, across the front seat, tied with a reef knot. I would have been a little wary if the journey was to be a couple of miles spent like this, let alone the daunting prospect of some 200 miles-plus held inside a battered tin can secured by a single strand of washing line. The spirit of the adventurer in me must have won through because, it was some hours later that I found myself being driven into an old farmyard, in complete darkness, by Larry, the ever optimistic one. We were greeted, after finally working out how to undo the knot in the rope across our laps, no mean feat in the dark, by a decrepit old farmer. Stating who he was, and that he had phoned earlier that day, Larry tried to strike up conversation with the ancient yokel. The old lad informed us that he himself, only lived there, and it was his son who ran the business from the outbuilding, and, he would not be there until Monday morning, today was Saturday. Larry had 'starred' once more I thought, and I went back to the car, leaving him to chat to the old man. When Larry got back in the car he said that the old fellow had given him a name, Len Fanshaw, and an address some fifteen miles away where we might get what we were after.

An hour later, the earlier entrance duplicated, this time into a much bigger yard, though still in total darkness. There was a door in the far corner, which had a half-glass panel showing a dull light into the courtyard. We again extricated ourselves from the rope's embrace, and like a pair of mesmerised moths set off towards the door. Larry tapped on the glass portion of the door, it was answered by a very large man about fifty with a totally bald head. Larry asked for Mr Fanshaw, we were duly invited in with a wave of 'baldies' hand. My eager companion proceeded to relay our intentions to this man of few words, in point of fact he didn't speak until Larry had finished. I must admit that from the moment we had walked through the door I thought I sensed something was not quite right. Baldy said only three words, "are you bogies?" (Bogies we later discovered was the local name for the police.) At which point he turned around and took from a drawer, what I can only describe as the biggest meat cleaver I have ever seen in my life. "I've had enough of you lot" he growled without even waiting for an answer to his question. Now I'm no coward, but faced with the prospect of me filling a case of dog food, I was joining Larry in the fastest 100 yards dash in living memory. Larry scorched out of the yard with the car as if our lives depended on it, (probably true). As we weaved our way to the main road, with both front doors flapping likes bees' wings, there was a loud bang at the back end. What a time to get a blow-out I thought, so I suspect did Larry, but puncture or not Larry was not stopping for man nor beast.

When I finally succeeded in making Larry stop to survey the damage, what we believed to be a puncture was in reality no such thing. The bang we heard was caused by no blow-out, our inspection of the car revealed a gash nine inches in length in the boot lid. This little episode, and our fruitless journey, had taught me a valuable lesson – never talk to strange men; especially if they are sporting a sharp instrument.

I didn't ask Larry how he explained the new ventilation hole in his mate's boot lid, in fact if the truth be known, I didn't much care either. Some weeks after Larry came around clutching yet another copy of the Meat Trades Journal. This time it was not to coax me into some prospect-less 'scam', but to show me an article relating to a court case, in which a farmer/wholesale butcher had received two year's imprisonment and phenomenal fines, for his involvement in the sale of £1,000,000 worth of knacker meat, to catering firms throughout the south of England. His name was Leonard Fanshaw aged 51. No wonder he was a little upset when Larry and I called that fateful night. He obviously thought we were indeed police, trying, so he probably thought, to gain further evidence against him. If his aim was better on the night we called he might in fact have been facing a far graver charge than he was in consequence sentenced for.

I wonder whether the old boy at the first farm, knew what manner of reception, Mr Fanshaw would greet us with – if he did, he had a lot more cunning than we gave him credit for. Being a life-long cynic I tend to think that he did.

This was definitely, positively, my last flirtation with the meat trade.

Footnote: Shamus, a little later in his career, managed to train a greyhound Derby winner – Lord help him if ever the N.G.R.C. ever heard of his 'flapping' interests. It could prove very embarrassing in some circles if my encounter with Shamus became public knowledge. Was my deal with him the only one, or did he conduct his business in underhand ways on more than one occasion?

I think not!

CHAPTER 3

I now return to the world in which I found it a lot easier to make money, <u>cars</u>, the lazy man's way to cash.

The first impression a punter gets can be crucial in the eventual sale of a banger, or indeed any car. If it looks well, and <u>seems</u> to go well, then you have a strong likelihood of achieving a sale. I shall deal for the moment with the a car's bodywork. The first thing a punter notices is, if the car looks good it creates the feeling of well being. Most victims sub-consciously or consciously make up their mind about whether or not to buy a car purely on it's appearance alone. Bodywork, even with no mechanical knowledge at all, is something anyone can tell the state or – or can they?

Although the successful *shearer* strives to buy a car for resale with decent bodywork, mainly for the reason described previously, when looking for a good selling prospect this is not paramount in his thoughts. The state of a car's exterior can be disguised with considerable ease – more to the point, with very little cost.

A form of hole covering, especially good for hiding cracks and holes in badly corroded chassis, sills, boot floors, inner wings etc, (in short anything needing welding for a correct repair which could prove very expensive and time consuming) most competent 'con' artists use a technique I term 'paper welding'. This involves measuring the area to be 'welded' and cutting a piece of newspaper slightly larger. Then mix up a small amount of body filler. Spread the filler thinly on the reverse side of the newspaper, covering it completely. The patch is now stretched over the hole and gently moulded to the contour required by hand. When this patch is set and has hardened it will give the appearance, once painted with underseal, of a neatly welded plate of metal. Although the 'repair' looks, and if felt, resembles a competent repair it's load bearing capacity is virtually nil – but the deception could be adequate to sell an otherwise, scrapyard prospect. All this is presuming that the car is in possession of a current M.O.T. No self-respecting con-man would buy a car without an M.O.T., unless the prospects for the car looked promising. (I shall discuss the easy way to M.O.T cars, quite legally of course, later on.) 'Paper welding' would suffice to tidy up the parts of a car not requiring paintwork, a greater amount of deception is required for this. Paintwork can be an expensive hobby both for trade and the private punter alike. For instance. a correct paint job needs, paint, thinners, maybe such items as lacquers and isolators depending on the type of paint used. For a full respray the cost can be prohibitive for just the paint etc, let alone the spraying equipment required to apply the said paint. If the 'con-man' were to use conventional methods therefore his profit would suffer dire consequences. At the time of writing the approximate cost, at trade prices, of materials for respraying an average family car was (depending on the quality of paint you use) anything from £60 to £200 to produce a reasonable finish that is.

I and countless friends in the banger trade, utilised a very much cheaper and easier method of respraying a car. The ugliest bodywork could be transformed quite cheaply, and thereby make a tidy saving on costs, increasing your profit margin.

The method is really simple, after the application of body filler to the worst parts of the bodywork and the subsequent masking up of the vehicle, respray needs no further preparation except a 'flatting down'. The paint used is any tin of household gloss, in any colour that takes your fancy. The thinners of a 'normal' respray are replaced with, petrol, (yes petrol), a gallon will suffice. The total cost of the 'con-man's' materials then is approximately the cost of 1 litre of household gloss plus 1 gallon of petrol. (And no, it doesn't matter whether it's leaded or unleaded, to you cynics out there.)

The paint is applied in one coat (unlike conventional cellulose paint) thinned just enough to pass through the spray gun. The car must then be left overnight in the garage, as the drying time is akin to normal house paint. The resultant finish is very good, giving a glass like shine needing no cutting back. To the unsuspecting punter – a lovely looking car. With this method none of the all-too-common reactions with old paintwork underneath are experienced, and so less risk of extra expense correcting paint jobs that have gone wrong. The eventual finished article is quite acceptable. It goes without saying though that this method would be a little coarse for anything more than a banger.

This particular story concerns a car I purchased from a neighbour. The car in question incidentally needed no doctoring at all by 'yours truly'. My neighbour was something of a D.1.Y. man, although only 20 years old he was quite proficient, I must admit. The car that I purchased from him, with the sole intention of re-selling it, was a Hillman Avenger 1500 G.L.S., a very fair car really. (I did a few nice ones.) It was taxed and tested, had tidy bodywork, and was a good runner. I bought the car for £100, he wanted considerably more, but I had worked out quite easily that he was broke. One of my motto's is 'take no prisoners' and so I'm afraid once my analysis of his situation was complete he had to suffer the consequences. Neighbour or no neighbour £100 was my offer he either took it or remained skint, needless to say he took it.

I duly advertised the car and sold it, without spending any money on it, for £250 – a bargain. The new owner was living in the next village and really pleased with his purchase, another satisfied customer, or so I thought.

I received a phone call some four hours after cash had changed hands and the punter seemed somewhat anxious as he said, "Hello, this car you sold to me." "Yes" was my reply. "I was showing it off to my son-in-law, and he says, the registration is not the right one." "Of course it is, it's the one on the registration document, and on the M.O.T. certificate, as well as the tax disc," I said with great confidence. Because I must admit I was a little confused as to where this was leading to. The agitated punter then said "I know but those documents and the registration number belong to a car my son-in-law sold to a garage three months ago, and not this car. This car is a lot better than the one he sold, and anyway his was only a 1500 DL, not a 1500 GLS as this one is."

My immediate thought was to say well what are you complaining about if you say it's so good, but I was only too aware of this particular *screamers* anguish, and I did not wish to worsen things by being witty at the wrong time. Besides this could have, if not handled right, nasty repercussions. I therefore said I would check with the guy I had bought it from and ring him back.

I walked down the street to have a word with Paul Middleton, the neighbour who had sold me the offending vehicle. No one in. I phoned the punter back to inform him of this, (the main point here was to keep the situation contained and not to let him panic and bring in the law). I was slightly taken aback by his reply, "Well if you give me my money back and take the car I'll not say any more about it, I don't want to get mixed up in this business, it's illegal you know, to swap around registrations.'

The fellow was obviously crapping himself over the affair. Assuring him that I'd sort it out I hung up, with the promise that I'd get back to him within the hour. This called for some serious thought. After a while I decided upon this course of action. Obviously I was not going to give him his money back, and be stuck with a car I couldn't sell on. That would mean I would have to give it back to our Mr Middleton and make no profit for myself – that would never do.

Well let's summarise, firstly the car was obviously a 'ringer'. (To cut a long story short, a car with a chassis number that does not tally with the one on the registration document.) Secondly. the details must have been changed during the last three months. I knew that the car had been in Paul Middleton's possession for about that length of time. Therefore the chances were, that he was indeed the culprit.

This being so, <u>he</u> was going to be the loser in this fiasco, not me. I again walked up the street and tried his door, where he lived with his parents. The door opened, it was his father, he asked me in, I then proceeded to tell him the tale. I added that I found myself unable to pay the punter his money back, as I had already spent it. (So my story was.) Mr Middleton senior very soon realised the gravity of the situation, and the urgency in retrieving the car before it turned into a police matter with the absent Middleton junior up to his neck in excrement. To rescue his wayward lad therefore he took it upon himself to pay the 'screamer' his money and take custody of the fated Avenger. Such a convincing story of doom and gloom that I had instilled upon him prompted him to virtually beg me to say nothing of the affair to anyone. Which I was only to pleased to do, after all I was £150 richer, a small price to pay, I would have thought, to preserve the family honour. (I deserve a medal.) It was the least I could do.

I never saw the car again or should I say cars, as it was really an illegal hybrid of two separate cars, again. The Middletons moved away not long after this little affair. Shame really I wouldn't have minded another car like that, but somehow it didn't look as though there would ever be the chance of a repeat performance from Middleton junior I wonder why?.

Some months later the truth of the matter came to light. Apparently junior had originally purchased the first car from the garage, that my punter's son-in-law had sold it to. A friend of Mr Middleton Snr, was selling a similar car – the 1500 G.L.S. for spares, it seemed that the G.L.S. had no M.O.T. but had plenty of good spares. Middleton Snr being a frugal man bought the said car, hoping to save his son a lot of future expense, Middleton Jnr, seeing that the car his father had bought was in a lot better condition than the one he himself had purchased, had a bright idea of making one good car out of two, nothing wrong in that you may say, and I would agree. Having decided that the G.L.S. had better bodywork and a lot nicer car all round, than his original acquisition, he took it upon himself to make the G.L.S. his dream car. The car purchased from the garage was to be then the 'donor' of parts to the GLS. (What a role reversal.) Nothing wrong with this, if the finished car is duly M.O.T. tested and taxed with the appropriate Registration number. Junior must, at some point in the process of producing his dream car, realised that, as the car bought for spares did not possess a current M.O.T. or Road Tax, he must, before venturing on to the public highway, acquire the aforementioned, for the resultant new vehicle. Now Middleton junior, being an enterprising young man, and a bit skint, hit upon the idea of using the M.O.T certificate and tax disc from the 'donor' vehicle, and to make the job complete, swap the registration plates as well. Wasn't he a clever boy then? (Talk about gifted amateurs.) I suppose he was lucky that I bought the car and not some more law-abiding citizen, otherwise I don't think he would have been so easily let off.

Still on the subject of 'Avengers' I had advertised and sold, some six months after the Middleton affair, another 'Avenger'. I had sold a lot of cars in between, but this particular car, and the circumstances surrounding it, stick in my memory. Not so much for the man I sold it to, but concerning one of the people I <u>didn't</u> sell it to. Confused? Then I shall explain. As is usual, once a car is sold, one can still receive phone calls from other prospective punters, who are unaware that the vehicle has been sold. One of these too-late punters was a gentleman, and I use the term 'gentleman' very loosely, named Mr Rothman, or so he said. The conversation went thus. "Hello, I'm ringing about your dear little car, the Avenger, is it still for sale?" asked the caller in a very camp, effeminate voice. "I'm sorry it's sold," I stated, wondering what the caller looked like with a voice like that. "Oh dear that is such a shame, was it a nice car," came the equally camp reply.

Thinking, to have a bit of fun I proceeded to sing the car's praises. (In truth it wasn't that bad a car really, but not as good as I was making it out to be.) After a very convincing description of the vehicle by 'yours truly', the same camp voice said, "Ohhhhh that sounds just lovely, oh I do wish I had bought it, it sounds like just the car I'm looking for."

For a moment I thought all this was one big wind up, by a friend or someone I knew. However he seemed like he may be a genuine – a proper 'shirt-lifter' in fact.

Well, as I have stated previously in this book, I'm not prejudiced and so I thought, what the hell? Take this wally's number, you may find another car to sell to him. 'Shirt-lifter' or not his money will spend just the same as anyone else's.

I therefore told him that I thought a friend of mine might be able to fix him up with a car, and duly said that he would call me the following day, he couldn't leave a number because he was not on the telephone at home, and could not leave his office number as he was at present on holiday, and would not return to work until the following week. He phoned me next day eager for news of a car for him. I hadn't been able to find a suitable motor, or at least one I could make decent profit on. I therefore told him that I was unable to get hold of my friend at the present time. He said that it was quite alright and that he didn't mind waiting for a good car. He gave me his office telephone number, complete with the extension to ask for, with the request I call when I had succeeded in contacting my man.

I didn't bother looking for a suitable car, as I had plenty more punters eager to press bundles of notes into my hand. He lived some distance away, why should I make the effort for a 'shirt-lifter' I thought. After selling a couple more re-vamped wrecks, I quite by chance came upon a nice looking Avenger, 'Shirt-lifter Sammy' (as I had nicknamed him at the time), came to mind as a likely punter. I also had a chance to satisfy my mild curiosity, as to what this camp talking fellow looked like. I had visions of a cross between Quentin Crisp and Larry Grayson, eventually meeting my gaze. Searching for the number he had given me a week before, I thought of all the usual cliches associated with dealings of this sort. (Better have an extra zip put in your trousers, at the back) and (make sure you take enough Vaseline with you, he might take a bit of persuading). I dialled the number, it was answered by a female voice, "Good morning, Sheffield City Council, can I help you?" My thoughts were interrupted by another female voice saying "Good morning. Consumer advice." Instinct told me to hang up quick-smart.

Well, was the whole thing a wind up, or did Mr Rothman just happen to work in the Trading Standards Department of Sheffield City Council. I tend to think it was a wind up, if it wasn't, I certainly was not going to court disaster by actually selling the man a car. It would be like giving your worst enemy a loaded gun and then telling him to fire it at you. The wind up was not the creation of anyone I knew, as a trick such as that, and it's all too many comical implications, would certainly have been made common knowledge throughout the local motor trade.

More than likely it was the effort of a member of the public, a wierdo, that got their kicks from doing such things. There are unfortunately, quite a few of them out there. Larry in point of fact pulled such a wierdo when selling a car of his through the same classifieds. The car in question was a black Capri, he asked me to help him formulate an advertisement that would make his car stand out from the rest. (A common ploy – it has the effect of people calling your number first, as your car would seem, at first glance, a better prospect than the other more mundane somewhat bland advertisements).

We made up an advertisement something along the lines of;

BEAUTIFUL BLACK CAPRI, taxed and tested, chrome wide wheels, stereo radio cassette, cloth upholstery, spot lights, etc, etc, first to see will buy, **NO DREAMERS PLEASE. £600.**

The above advertisement was phoned through for inclusion in the Cars For Sale, section of the local evening paper, by hopeful Larry. It would, we presumed appeal to the 'go faster-cum-poser brigade', and the adage 'no dreamers' designed to put off the inevitable, time-wasting, pimple-faced youth with an old battered Escort and very little cash, trying to 'pinch' the car. There are lots of 'dreamers' out there believe it or not, that actually rate their heaps of junk at ridiculously high prices. This is I believe the fault of people like myself, for fooling them into believing the wreck that you are selling them is worth a lot more than it really is. A fact of life in the motor trade is; A car is only worth what someone is willing to pay for it. For example if a mug says his car is worth £1,000 and all he can manage to get for it is £800 then the logic is obvious, would you not say? Not so, in the mind of the average punter he has let his car go for less than it is worth. This then is the challenge faced by the motor dealer when allowing for part exchange, I don't know many punters who rate their cars at a lower price than they paid for it, but the truth is that at least 80% of second hand cars sold today are sold at a greater price than their actual 'market value', yet still the vast majority of the car owning public overate the car they currently own. So the term 'dreamers' can cover a multitude of punter types. One other thing to complicate the issue is the fact that whether they are or not, no one actually believes that the term applies to them. All too often, the very people that do think it doesn't apply to them, are the worst offenders.

As Larry was not on the telephone, he placed the advertisement, using my number. The Capri sold to the second punter but the calls kept coming in. One such call was made by what can only be described, as an old woman not in full possession of her faculties or in more common terminology, 'a few sandwiches short of a picnic', or 'not playing with a full deck'. Upon answering the phone I was greeted by the following,

"Hello I'm ringing about your car, I don't want to buy it." Rather cheeky of you I thought.

"No dreamers indeed. I bet you're sorry about that aren't you?"

She then burst into song– a term I use very loosely:

> "I'm a dreamer
> I dream all day,
> I'm a dreamer,
> Take my car away,
> I don't want it,
> So take it away,
> I'm a dreamer,
> I dream all day".

I asked, "Who is this?" adding "You're crackers, woman"

"Owwwww, yes wouldn't you like to know?"

She was now cackling like an old witch, and then she started singing her 'song' again. I quickly handed the telephone to Larry – after all, if I told him afterwards about her, he might not have believed me. She cackled on for about three minutes in total. We didn't mind it was her money. She eventually hung up after yet another chorus of 'I'm a dreamer'. Larry and I were in fits of laughter by this time. It brings to mind the saying, 'it takes all sorts to make a world' after this particular rendition my opinion is – it certainly does.

I now come to an incident relating to myself and an M.O.T. testing station. I had purchased an Escort with very good bodywork, from a local car auctions. The engine was not bad, for an Escort, unfortunately there was no current M.O.T. on the vehicle. But at the bargain price of £60 I thought it a relatively safe gamble in purchasing it. I set about the task of 'repairing it'.

The main problems were, brakes, tyres, and track rod ends, plus a fair amount of welding. The welding I could not bodge (not for an M.O.T. test anyway) but I was not going to be stung 'an arm and a leg' for new brakes, tyres and track rod ends. The new cost of parts needed was somewhere in the region of £100. In the event, the cost of parts to bring the car up to M.O.T. standard came to the veritable king's ransom of £4.00. The way that I achieved this is simple – the car was sent, (I couldn't take it myself as I was known to this testing station. I had not done anything personally to them, but my reputation was all too well known to them), for an M.O.T. test with all the faults still on the car. The reasons for this are:

a) You would receive a failure sheet naming all the faults they had found. This meant that you did not have to carry out any un-necessary work, all that you wanted was a pass certificate not a medal for conscientious working.

b) The tester would only check that, the faults he initially failed the car on, had been rectified, meaning that, certain faults he may have missed, if any, during his first examination would not be, if all went well, discovered on the second examination. (The re-test).

A common belief amongst most members of the public, is that if a car fails on any particular part, the offending part, in order to pass the M.O.T. must be replaced with a new one. Not so. Let me first take the brakes on the said Escort. This particular model had drum front brakes. When testing brakes of this type the method of testing is such that all the testing station actually does is to test the efficiency of the brakes – and no inspection of the state of the linings of the said brakes takes place. In other words the brake linings could in theory be almost worn out and still pass the test. Nevertheless the efficiency of the Escort's brakes was well below the standard required to pass the test first time. No great surprise to me actually, inspection of the linings upon the car's return from the test revealed that they were indeed completely worn out. The solution – not new linings, but second-hand ones from your friendly neighbourhood scrapyard.

The new set of four brake shoes were a might expensive at £1 per pair don't you think? Sod the expense I thought, and duly fitted them in place of the original linings. The brakes passed the re-test with flying colours, for a fraction of the new price. The track rod ends were also worn out and so similar replacement with second-hand ones was carried out, resulting in a pass, at the magnificent price of £1.00 the three tyres were even cheaper. I didn't even have to buy any. Larry and quite a few friends incidentally, were running at the time Ford cars. I therefore borrowed three of Larry's wheels and tyres for an hour. (Almost all Fords e.g. Escorts, Cortinas, Capris and Sierras use wheels of the same size and are interchangeable.) The escort went back for the test, and of course passed. One minor thing, which the tester had missed on his second examination, was that I had by accident burnt through a seat belt whilst doing the welding required, rendering it useless. I sold the car, complete with a full year's test for £400, to a Mrs Royal. I heard nothing about the car for three days. When the statutory phone call came, and she was screaming that I had sold her a car with bald tyres and a useless seat belt, which probably meant she said "That it's got one of those there 'bent' M.O.T.'s I've heard about." I said if she thought that to be the case she had better take it up with the testing station, as, far as I was concerned, in my view everything was all above board. As the law stood it was the testing station that was at fault, and not me. Even though I had swapped the tyres, there was nothing she could do to me as I was in possession of a 'get out of jail free card', meaning that I was a 'private man' and we all know the situation by now as far as the law and the 'private man' is concerned. She may scream a little as the majority do, but she would drop it when she saw that her chances of success were nil.

I had when I sold her the car given her, the old bailiff's routine. Even though I was by this time, living a fairly comfortable lifestyle, complete with a Jaguar XJ6, which I was running at the time. My excuses made in the usual traditional fashion – she took her complaint, of which I was completely unaware, to the M.O.T. testing station. The tester himself asked (so I am reliably informed), where she had purchased the car, and when my name was revealed, Graham, (the tester) to put it mildly was not amused. At this point a brief interpretation of the legislation regarding the granting of an M.O.T. certificate seems appropriate. The tester grants a certificate, saying that the items tested were correct on the day that he tested them. The exact wording, to be found on the reverse side of any M.O.T. Test Certificate states;

> This certificate relates only to the condition of the testable items at the time of the test. It should not be regarded as evidence to the condition of the items tested at any other time nor should it be taken as evidence of the general mechanical condition of the vehicle.

(This little snippet of legislation gives people like myself a licence to 'con'.)

Although this is all correct, in my experience, no self-respecting M.O.T. testing station is going to jeopardise their livelihood by sticking rigidly to this statement. So poor Graham, to prevent our lovely Mrs Royal going over his head to the Ministry of Transport to complain, has to shell out for three brand new tyres and a new seat belt. Whilst he was fitting the aforementioned, he informed Mrs Royal that I was in fact, a motor dealer and not as I had informed her on the breadline. Graham it seems was trying to effect some form of revenge by imparting this information to her. What constantly amuses me is or rather was the pathetic attempts, by both general public and a few members of the trade, to bring me to book. Without boasting, not one of the attempts has succeeded, as I always remained one step in front of any such eventuality, this is the difference between 'the professional' and those that just think they are a professional. Later on I shall tell of other like-thinking individuals all of them failed. Naturally.

After Graham had finished 'singing my praises' Mrs Royal duly telephones me to remonstrate saying "Hello Mr Milton how's your

Jaguar?" I replied "Fine thanks how's your little Escort?" She was after this remark, rather rude to 'yours truly'. Oh I was upset.

Graham was too much of a sheep to bother contacting me about the affair, he obviously knew that it would have been a fruitless pursuit anyway. At least he had been taught a lesson from it all, Lord help anyone taking a car to him for a test, hoping for him to be a little lenient. I ought to be given a job by the Ministry of Transport, checking the laxity of testing stations. (That was a joke – honest!)

Still on the subject of practising the art, that brings to mind a short story about the totally illegal practice of 'clocking'. A trade associate of mine recently told me of an incident, which serves to indicate the scale of the enterprise.

We are all led to believe that 'clocking', is not a widespread problem in the motor trade. My thirty odd years in the trade suggest otherwise. Before I go any further I shall explain, to those of you who are unfamiliar with the phrase, or what 'clocking' entails. The mileage of a car is one of the premier factors relating to the second-hand value of it, the lower the amount of miles a car has driven, the higher it's second-hand value is. Therefore the discerning punter searches for the lowest mileage he can find, thereby ensuring a less worn-out car. Normally the aforementioned would be a reasonable assumption that is, if the mileage reading shown on the speedometer is indeed correct. In my experience at the more 'dodgy' end of the market, (where most 'bargains' are to be found), the vast majority of cars, have, at some-time, had the odometer reading altered. This is a relatively simple procedure for the able mechanic, and could be the greatest contribution to the car's resale value. Without going into too much technical detail, the job entails the removal of the main instrument panel, in the majority of cases anyway, to gain access to the speedometer odometer counter.

The incident I referred to earlier involved a Mercedes saloon, of some eight years of age. After removing the instrument panel, my friend noticed a folded piece of paper attached to the back of the speedometer by masking tape. After detaching the tape he unfolded the paper, it had written on it the words 'Oh no not again!'

The car had quite obviously been the victim of a 'mileage clockers screwdriver' before, and it was about to suffer the same fate again.

One must feel a certain amount of pity for the poor unsuspecting punter, who eventually was to be the next proud owner of the Mercedes. (Sad to say he is not the only one.) He would be driving a car, that in point of fact, had covered something like 60.000 miles or so, more than he was aware of, and more to the point, would have paid a vast amount more than it's true value, when he handed over his 'folding stuff'.

There is no one certain method of ensuring whether a particular car has been 'clocked' or not. There are a few ways of being pretty sure, these include, buying a car with a full and comprehensive service history, also one can be reasonably certain if the previous owner on the registration document is the only one and just happens to possess all the relevant service documentation from new. In general though, if 'clocking' is carried out by a competent person, on a suitable vehicle, it would be very hard to detect, in fact nigh on impossible in some cases.

As the average yearly mileage of any car is judged to be between, 10,000 and 12,000 miles, the removal of a few years mileage by 'clocking' can both increase it's market value, and improve it's chances of selling. The 'clocking' of a car above ten years old is a relatively rare occurrence, although it is, and has been done in order to enhance it's saleability, especially if the condition of the car is such that, 'it would stand it' in other words a low mileage would not look out of keeping with the cars condition. By the time a car has reached ten years old it may well have had it's mileage altered more than once, as it could quite conceivably have passed through the hands of 'clockers' a number of times during those 10 years.

The whole business of 'clocking' and it's ease of execution, and if done competently, it's virtual impossibility to detect, displays yet another example of the advise to be heeded of.

BUYER BEWARE.

I can say, with my hand on my heart, that I found no need to 'clock' any car that passed through my hands. After all, I could make money by other deceptive methods, I therefore left the art of 'clocking' to the <u>honest</u> car dealers, if there was such a thing that is.

The gullibility of Joe Public knows no social or intellectual barriers. I have stung people from most sectors of the social scene, from college lecturers and teachers (these are in my opinion the most naive of the group), right down to the lowly dole merchant. From members of the trade (yes even certain members of this particular group have fallen prey to my methods), to policemen. I've sold cars (not all of them wrecks), to anyone clutching the necessary, <u>cash</u>.

To sell to the likes of the, so-called academics, I found all too easy. They may have been educationally superior, to the average man, but when confronted by a streetwise, intellectual equal, ME, (conceited bastard aren't I?), the result was inevitable. The problem, from their point of view, was the limited technical knowledge that they tended to be in possession of (perhaps they should do their homework a little better, – a joke, get it? Ah well), especially when it came to salient points relating to the engines etc. Talk about lambs to the slaughter. There was the occasional exception, but these were very few and far between, and as the saying goes there were plenty 'more fish in the sea'. It was nice to sell your car to the first punter that came along, but it little mattered whether it was the first, second or third or even more that eventually parted with the readies. The important thing was that <u>someone</u> eventually <u>did</u> hand over the all- powerful folding stuff. In my opinion there is a punter for every car on the road (or off it for that matter). The skill was in matching one with the other. This job was carried out by Yours Truly, in numerous ways, the easiest way of all of course was to <u>lie</u>. Because of the abundance of punters out there, the result of one's efforts was soon realised, if only one knew what you were doing. Over the years there have been many people that have attempted to emulate my successful efforts. After all I did make it look easy. To the un-initiated it looked dead simple. All they thought you had to do was to trot along to the car auctions and buy any car that took their fancy, and advertise it at a profit, and sit back. They just had to wait for the money to come falling into their laps. If I had to be pound for every single one of these 'copy cats' I would certainly have been a very wealthy man by now. Most of the failed 'copy cats' sub-scribed to the theory that if you fork out enough you'll get a good car. A similar theory to 'you get what you pay for' – not so, especially when buying at car auctions. As the greater part of my emulators found out, the price you may pay at auction is not indicative of its condition. A few of them thought, quite rightly, that a knowledge of car mechanics, may provide some assistance. True, a mechanic might help you buy a reasonably sound car, but whether or not you managed to get it at a price low enough to resell it for profit, now that was another matter. The main reason for this being, that if you see a good prospect, the odds are greatly in favour of other people noticing the said car also. The biggest danger of all is that a private punter might spot the car, he after all said and done, is not out to buy a car to resell. The outcome usually means that the private punter bids a lot higher than is possible to make profit, and so disappears your prospect.

After all this, you get a car good enough to resell but the greatest task of all is ahead of you. That is – to finally sell it for profit. There are a lot of people out there who can repair cars, and can also buy a good car, but there are not many guys out there, capable of, let alone daring enough, to sell cars on a scale such as I was doing. Ask any member of the public if they could see themselves carrying out such an occupation, with all it's risks and pitfalls, and I don't think you would get many takers. Joe Public is an animal that likes to earn his money by more conventional, safer, means. (Well most of them do).

By far the greatest attribute a car salesman can have, is the ability to listen. At first hand you may disagree saying his ability to talk be paramount. The truth is if he is not a good listener, how will he know where to target his conversation for the best result? Every good salesman knows to be true.

Joe Public, although easily taken in, (well most of you are), always has at the back of his mind, especially when buying a second hand car, the thought, 'is he ripping me off? The individual's brain may not conjure up those exact words, but if one is to credit the victim with even the smallest of sense, a phrase of some similar type is bound to cross his mind at some point in the proceedings. The blame for this moment of trepidation lies, so I think, at the door of such consumer programmes such as 'That's Life' and '4 what it's worth' plus the numerous magazines currently being sold, with the poor innocent consumer in mind. The efforts of the aforementioned T.V programmes, and publications have very little effect, indeed the enterprising salesman can turn such information as is proffered by them, to his advantage. Well I could and so I don't see why any <u>good</u> salesman should be concerned by their existence. The alert con-man can instinctively recognise any mental resistance to his aims, simply by his victims manner and his tone of speech. The messages that he receives via his victims body language, at various points during an attempted sale, will provoke the required response from the salesman. A <u>good</u> salesman does not lose many sales, or at least I didn't, and I am by no means unique. Although this was usually the case, there could be a few exceptions. One of these, in fact, the most common, is a punter 'without the were with all' (skint). The fact that he is, broke, does not, as you may think, put this type of punter off. He more than likely possesses a little money, but not the sum required to buy your car. He seems to be under the illusion that he will be able to barter with you in an effort to get you to accept considerably less than you first hoped for. This ploy might work with your average Joe Soap type of vendor, but not I'm afraid with anyone else. This type of punter must not be confused with the supposedly 'streetwise' clever sod. Who probably has the full asking price of the car in his pocket, but is trying to show you how good he is at bargaining. Experience tells how to distinguish between the two. The first type of punter is a total waste of time, as if you are to make a profit, you are not going to let the car go for the price he would be likely to offer. He is the original 'time waster'. This type of punter can be linked to another sort, the 'joy rider', usually a young lad who turns up in answer to an advert you may place, offering a high performance car. The lad turns up in something like an old Escort or a Datsun Cherry, his pockets are empty, but at least he can say to his mates he was thinking of buying your 'posers dream'. It serves to give him street cred with his mates. His excuse for not buying it, to his mates that is, is probably because of some imaginary fault he happened to invent. Still he did show his intention to buy the car, or so he'd like his mates to believe. Even though he didn't or should I say <u>couldn't</u> buy the car his street cred is increased 200%. His friends (he hoped) would be saying "hey up

Garry was going to buy that RS 2000 in the paper you know, but he said it was too rough so he didn't bother". Instant admiration from his associates who probably only drive round in lowly Fiestas, Minis or VW Polos. This situation occurs all too often, it is one thing to desire a particular car that is advertised, but quite another to actually afford it, as anyone can tell you. But the young lad could step up in the pecking order, if he went to look at a few although he could never afford one. (But his mates didn't know that). Maybe if he found a vendor daft enough, he might even get to test drive his dream car. (Probably giving himself a multi-orgasm in the process). Now wouldn't that increase his 'street cred'.

I could go into the psychology of *shearing* and fill a whole book. But, even though it plays a major role in any con, it soon becomes boring to talk about, especially for you, the reader anyway. We shall therefore go on to the next phase of my practical career training. This portion of my 'education' will, more than likely, take up the rest of this book, as it was the greatest two years of my life to date.

Conning was soon to be carried out by me on a far greater scale than even I, expected. The beauty of it all was that it would all be done quite legally, as I have always endeavoured to do, naturally. Financially this stage of my career was to be a very rewarding one, and socially very good. I met and made a tremendous amount of friends in the two years. But far and away the most important thing about this period of time was that, it was great fun.

The source of all this fun, and the start of something that people of Chesterfield had never before experienced, or for that matter were likely to again, was the birth of Bill's Bangers. (Not the real name of the place but the name still portrays the type of company it was). A friend in the trade, a *shearer* like myself, (but nowhere near as skilful, in my opinion) came into a little money. We were partaking of the old liquid refreshment one day and the conversation came around to the usual, cars.

I said, that I had always wanted, (what most banger lads did) a pitch of my own. I wanted a pitch with a difference, instead of the usual run of the mill middle range of cars, (a trade term relating to cars, not too cheap, and not too expensive, hence, middle range) I would fill such a pitch with, bangers. I was unaware of my drinking partner's recent legacy at this time. Until of course Pete, (Peter Alan Day to give him his full title), informed me of his windfall. When he did in fact tell me of his good fortune, I am afraid the *shearer* in me took over. I became intent therefore of persuading Pete to grant me my wish. I have the enviable ability, no not ability, the skill, of convincing people to follow a plan I wish them to follow. The reason I call it skill, is the fact that I always succeed in putting it in such a way that they indeed think it their own idea – the ultimate weapon for a con-man. My skill was employed to good effect on Pete, he soon came up with this brilliant idea, 'why don't we start a pitch selling bangers. I said (as part of my plan of course), "just as soon as I win the pools we'll start shall we". (So what if it wasn't that subtle, we were drunk you know). Trying to be somewhat witty he said "no need to wait I've as good as won them haven't I?".

Bill's Bangers was now more than just a dream to me – it was, if I played my cards right, about to become a definite reality. I could quite possibly have conned the £6,000 or so required from one source or other I suppose, but two things were evident to me at this moment in time. Number one was the prospect of the both of us making a fair amount of money out of the venture. Which meant that I did not need to work any form of scam to raise cash for the near future. Number two: I was going to have a lot of fun making it. There was no need therefore to risk a con when Pete was putting the required cash in the 'frame'. I was going to have the pleasure of running my 'own' car sales pitch, but more importantly, the way I had things worked out there were going to be no responsibilities for me to shoulder. (For example Tax, National Insurance etc). To achieve this state of affairs, without the objection of Pete was certainly going to take quite a fair amount of 'midnight oil burning' for Yours Truly in order for Bill's Bangers to come to life in the form that I had planned. I had set myself greater tasks in the past and so this was going to be no problem at all.

It came to pass, or so the saying goes, that we started to search for a car sales pitch. It was to prove a thankless occupation. The profession of car salesman was, it seemed one to be frowned upon. In the eyes of the local council you were classed one step below that of murderers and rapists. Therefore it soon became patently obvious that we were not going to be granted planning permission on any prospective site we came across. We had no chance then of getting Bill's Bangers off the ground, unless we could find a pitch, with the required planning authority intact. This turned out to be a lot harder than we first anticipated, as all the suitable sites we came up with, were already occupied. The search was entering it's third week, and Pete's enthusiasm was beginning to wane. I had to find a place fast, or risk the whole idea going down the pan. Just by chance, I was driving into town one day, and for no apparent reason, I found myself taking a turning into a road I had not driven on for years. (Slight exaggeration, but it sounds better than a few weeks.) On this road there was a set of temporary traffic lights, damn council creating work for their employees again, no doubt. Whilst waiting for them to change, (you always seem to hit these sort of lights when they are on red don't you?), I glanced at my surroundings, I was waiting outside of a yard with six foot chain link fence around it, and a set of double gates. It was being used, by the looks of it, as some sort of storage depot for a landscape gardener. I recognised the place as the old car sales where, some fifteen years previously I had bought my first really powerful car, a Ford Zodiac. (Now I'm showing my age.) Since that time it had been used for a number of purposes, log yard, builder's depot, a scrapyard and now a gardener's stockyard. The reason for the failure of the car sales, I presume, was, that some ten years ago the road it was on, had a bypass slice it into two, both the respective halves led directly to nowhere. The subsequent drop in trade resulting from a drastic reduction of passing vehicles, caused a previously thriving business to fail.

 Upon enquiries, quite discreetly made, about the actual law relating to planning permission, with particular interest to the old car sales, I discovered a fact that cheered me up no end. The original planning consent, on the pitch, was never changed – it was still down on record as car sales. Half my struggle was over, I had found the place that I had been seeking. All that remained was for me to get the current occupier to leave, and get the owner of the land to let us use it instead. I discovered that the owner of the said land was a car body repairer, a Mr Lang. His repair workshop was a recently built brick unit at the far end of the now defunct car sales site. The tenant of the rest of the land turned out to be a ferret-faced little man, of around thirty years of age and whose name was Nigel Hicks. In my pursuit of information I established that the landlord, our Mr Lang, was (like most men in the motor trade) a lover of the 'folding stuff'. It went without saying that my assault must, first and foremost be targeted on the greedy Mr Lang. After first pointing out to him that 'the ferret' only used some twenty-five per cent of the land I asked if it were possible for us to rent the unused section of land. At a comparative rent of course. Being the usually avaricious type, it was hard for our prospective landlord to disguise the look in his eyes when the prospect of doubling his income at no extra effort. I dispensed my telephone number, and asked him to call, after he had spoken with his current tenant about the matter. My proposal won through in double quick time, as he rang to confirm my assumptions within the hour.

The next obstacle to overcome was where was I to find the thirty or so bangers to fill the place? The most cars I had ever bought at any one time before, at auction was the grand sum of three. That week every car auction for a fifty mile radius, was paid a visit and as luck would have it, we managed the thirty cars we required.

My next step was to engage the services of a suitably experienced mechanic, his main attribute was to be that of being able to <u>bodge</u> a car rather than expensively repair it. In other words he had to have no scruples as far as the conning of Joe Public was concerned. What short cuts he didn't already know I was quite prepared to teach him.

A lot happened in the first week of trading at Bill's Bangers. The whole idea of a 'legal' sales pitch, selling nothing but old bangers went against the grain with the local council. We were after all, getting away with, and without penalty, the act of conning the local citizens out of their hard earned readies, and that would never do would it? What we were in fact doing was nothing different from what the 'private man' was doing, except we were doing it on a far larger scale. The council's policy must have been that it was alright for one man to sell one banger at a time, conning the public. But another thing for one man to sell twenty different cars to twenty different punters, (conning them nevertheless) and have the law descend upon him and punish him if any of those bangers were faulty. The 'private man', got away with it. Rather luckily so did I. Needless to say I took it upon myself to avenge the poor down-trodden motor dealer, and how I wreaked such vengeance.

The psychological rules of such a profession were adhered to quite undauntingly by myself. I was of the opinion that what would attract one punter could attract a dozen. Let's face it the average buyer (or should I say prospective buyer) of any banger has an open mind when faced with the numerous vehicles for sale. If the price is right, and the car looks a bargain, then they might consider a closer inspection. Let's just suppose that you were in search of a cheap car, a glance through the classifieds would possibly be your first course of action. This would entail listing the cars advertised in order of merit, and then visiting each one in turn. Hoping that, any particular car was to be acceptable, and more importantly, was still for sale, by the time you arrived to look at it. More than likely the car you were in fact most attracted to, would have been sold by the time you had got there. (As the chances are that any seemingly good car would attract the interest of others as well as yourself). this could mean that a whole weekend might be wasted, and still you may be devoid of transport.

Would not the ideal situation be if all the suitable bangers, in those classifieds, were pooled together for you to view at your leisure?

This idea would be great you may say. My aim was to give the prospective punter this type of opportunity. Experience has taught me that the average punter, given the choice, would prefer such a situation. I was therefore going to exploit this format to the limit. There is and always will be a thriving market for bangers. Ninety-five per cent of car dealers sell cars of the middle range and up. Yet I was to find that in the area where I lived, some fifty per cent of punters are looking for a banger as opposed to a more expensive mode of transport. A casual glance at the classifieds will reveal that at least seventy-five per cent of cars are usually of the higher priced end of the market (above £500) but at any given time there are only fifty per cent of the punters looking for such a higher priced vehicle. So it goes with out saying that there is twice the chance of selling a banger than a dearer priced car. The buyer of a banger in general, is not as 'fussy' as other punters – hence a better chance of achieving a sale. The aforementioned being so one would expect a few dealers than at present, would want to concentrate their efforts on the sale of bangers a little more. Fortunately for me they are not. The main reason being that, even though a vast majority of punters, who buy bangers, realise that they are not buying a <u>new</u> car, there are a few 'knob heads' who expect just that, in fact a <u>new</u> car for a few hundred quid. If the 'knob heads' find that when they get home, that they have not got a <u>new</u> car, but instead there are a few minor blemishes. They turn into the pathetic animal the *screamer*. This then is the main reason for any dealers apprehension about selling bangers. <u>Not me</u>. If I was to run this pitch successfully I had to find a way to pacify the inevitable screamers. This is how I did it, if a screamer came back with a genuine complaint, (I.E. one apertaining to the cars roadworthy condition) the fault was rectified, unless the expense was deemed too great. If this was the case then I would invite the punter to select another car, (for this to have a better effect I would offer him a (slightly) higher-priced car in place of the offending one). If the punter continued to *scream* after rectification of the fault, or would not take a replacement, I F****d him off, firstly making sure that any M.O.T testable item was adequately repaired. I used my discretion in every case of course, (believe it or not there weren't that many *screamers*) but <u>no one</u> repeat <u>no one</u> ever got their money back.

After all if anyone *screamed* to the Trading Standards, there was very little that they could do. I was therefore (I say this with tongue in cheek) akin to James Bond. He was <u>licensed to kill</u> and I was <u>licensed to con</u>. Make no bones about it there were no exceptions.

The phrase, 'All human life is here' carried a new meaning at Bill's Bangers, as some of the characters that came to inspect our vehicles could prove. Certain types of punter provoked me into attaching some very descriptive nicknames to my punters. The names I chose to give them were reflective of their, looks, actions and intellectual prowess. The biggest time wasters of all were 'knob heads', those just looking with no intention to purchase, were deemed 'spyers', and the opposite of course were 'buyers'. People who were a little harder to define were termed 'prospectives'. The lowest form of punter (both in looks and brains, ascertained usually by their words and actions) were to be known as 'pond life'. Ones patience was tried all too often by this abundant type. On the odd occasion we get a really gormless type of punter, I.Q. of about minus 200, were to be designated, 'plant life'. The most obvious 'plant life' were those witty folk just about able to say, 'Der, my brain 'urt's'. One of my usual forms of sales pitch was to lower or higher my tone of speech. If at all possible I would also tone down my intellectual status, in order to be on a level with my intended victim. It has become evident over the years that most people like to buy a car from someone of similar background and standing. I must ask you the reader, to try to visualise Yours Truly, attempting to give the impression of being on a par with a member of 'plant life' incorporated. Being in one's second childhood bore no resemblance I can assure you, but what the hell it was a good laugh. I did not, funnily enough, have any contempt for the 'pond and plant life' I came across, and you probably wouldn't believe me when I say that sometimes I regretted, (only for a fleeting moment mind), having to take advantage of such types but as I have explained before I am not prejudiced in my efforts. There was one type of punter that I took great pleasure in, 'pulling one over on', and that was the stuck up 'know all'. He thought he was the 'be all and end all' of mechanical knowledge. These were the most satisfying sort to 'rip off' as, to me, this kind of guy deserved everything he got.

There are some of you out there I am sure, that would class me as a condescending show-off And one of life's boasters. If I seem to be just this type, I must sincerely apologise, my intention in writing this book is merely to educate, and point out to the un initiated just how easy it is to con the all too gullible members of the public. To hope that by reading of my experiences, you do not suffer the same fate. I am, as the saying goes, 'a reformed character', and accordingly pose no further threat to the innocent members of out society. But I am afraid to say that my former profession is now experiencing something of an upturn and is something of a boom industry at the present time. The saying 'forewarned is forearmed' is the method by which I hope you, the reader, will learn. I know only too well that, due to the present hard times we find ourselves in, my former profession offers a very attractive, and lucrative, option to the boring hum-drum lives we are expected to lead.

From the day that I opened the gates for the first time, the powers that be tried their hardest to close us down. I foiled every attempt with comparative ease, after all the law is there for the protection of us all, not just the innocents amongst us. The majority of people hold the processes of the law in awe, scared stiff of it's consequences should they happen to fall foul of it. The law is nothing to be afraid of as long as you interpret it correctly and assess it's limitations and plan your intentions accordingly. This makes the difference between, in my case anyhow, between success and failure, and I had no desire to fail.

Within weeks of the commencement of our venture we were subject to a visitation by the local Trading Standards Department of the council. In their words it was just a 'routine' visit to assist us to trade in the correct manner — very thoughtful of them to think of us, and touching that they were concerned lest we should make any mistakes.

I was looking at the underside of an Escort estate, checking for any need for paper welding to it's chassis, when I glanced over to the gates. My view was such that I could see the lower part of two pairs of legs approaching the office, and walking to meet them was Pete's jeans lined pair of legs, I could just about make out the conversation as it went something like so;

One pair of legs said to Pete, "Good afternoon are you the owner". Pete replied "Well yes I suppose I am". Same pair of legs, "My colleague and I are from the Office of Fair Trading, I wonder if we could have a word regarding your invoices etc".

I had a faint recollection of having heard this voice before. I rose to my feet and before my eyes were the two Trading Standards Officers, that had, a few years earlier attempted to hang me out to dry over an incident concerning a white Ford Capri 3 Litre.

Pete was about to start up a conversation with the two undesirables, when I had cause to make them turn around, I shouted, "Pete don't even speak to those bastards, tell them to F*** off'.

The up till then silent one of the pair, stammered, "H-H-H-How l-l-l-long has Mr Milton b-b-b-been working here?"

I stated very loudly and with a marked degree of contempt, "long enough to know that you're wasting your time here, Now F*** off and don't come back."

They promptly obliged with my kind request, and swiftly made an exit.

I thought, smiling to myself, I bet they thought that they were going to put the person in charge of a place so aptly named as Bill's Bangers, well and truly straight on how to conduct his business. Until that is they discovered that it was me that they would be 'trying it on with'.

Any of the Trading Standards officers working locally must be aware of my reputation, and so it would take a brave man indeed to try and make any charge stick, in court. I feel sure that a fair number in their department would not be too willing to get egg on his face attempting to bring me to book. There were I am certain, far easier cases on their files. They could never hope to amass enough evidence to prosecute me successfully, I would have had to have been subjected to a lobotomy, before I was daft enough to fall into their hands. 'Once bitten – twice shy' was the phrase that came to mind at the time, so I recall. The Trading Standards Officers retired to a safe distance so to speak, and were to try other methods, in their attempt to prevent us trading — all of which were to subsequently fail, I shall come to their pathetic attempts later in the book, meanwhile onto the matter in hand – Bill's Bangers.

I wanted to attract as many punters as possible, for obvious reasons. The local papers were full of advertisements, both private and trade. To make the prospective victims out there sit up and take notice, I needed to make my advertisements stand out from the rest, (and remain in the thoughts of my intended victims). After a little deliberation and careful thought I formulated a way of achieving the required result. The following is a typical example of the advertisements that I was to place on a weekly basis in the largest of the local rags.

BILL'S BANGERS
FORGET THE REST COME
AND BE RIPPED OFF BY THE BEST

'W' Reg VW Scirocco in red, Tested 10 months, Taxed, once owned by local folk hero Pyclet Pete, so you'll have no problem pulling crumpet in this one lads, come and butter me up with £695.

'V' Reg Ford Cortina 1600GL Tested 7 months, complete with air-conditioned front wings if you can start it you can own it for £220

'X' Reg Fiat Panda, Taxed, Tested, Colour scheme makes it look like a fag packet, and it smokes a lot, but look at the price £295

'T' Reg Ford Escort 1300L estate, in a state, interior been savaged by a pair of mad dogs, big enough for a coffin, it's your funeral at £275

'V' Reg Fiat 126, Tested 11 months, what a little gem, runs on petrol fumes, looks like a fag-end come and stub it out for £265

Loads more heaps of junk to be sick of, on, or in. We even have a few good cars for sale. HONEST. Clean cars bought for cash (Not much). Come down and have a chat, we don't bite you know. Not yet

TELEPHONE ....

Something along these lines was placed in the local press, every week. Varying vehicles were described similarly to the aforementioned. It worked, every weekend we were flooded out with curious, prospective punters, all eager to meet and hopefully buy a car from, the man behind such original advertisements. I was not going to disappoint them.

CHAPTER 4

There were quite a few 'characters' in those first months of our venture. Pete did not concern himself with the day-to-day running of the business, he tended to wander about doing his 'projects'. These usually took the form of his version of a rally-prepared Escort. I was not averse to his 'hobby' as he was not interfering with the running of 'my pitch', and his projects did, eventually, become a saleable item. Most of the projects were standard 1300 Escorts with a 2000cc engine wedged in them, and a few other 'go faster' goodies stuck on. It kept him busy, and out of my way, as the best *shearers* like to work alone. (Mainly because there's no one else to stick his oar in and possibly ruin a good con.) In point of fact Pete was, in reality a shy lad. He was quite content for me to tackle the, sometimes, foreboding, onslaught of punters.

    I have discovered over the years that your average member of the public is, on first acquaintance, a very cautious and introvert animal. (Even though some may pretend otherwise.) This is the time for immediate action, the able *shearer* must, at the outset, put the punter at ease. After all, if you are to assess the victim correctly, in order to channel your sales pitch, you must first achieve some sort of repartee with him, (or indeed her). Every punter is a different individual, and so to enable you to sell to as many prospective customers as possible, it is imperative to break this first important barrier. The hardest work any salesman can experience is to attempt to sell some commodity to a man that is not responsive to any part of his efforts. The onus then, is on the salesman to 'open up' his prospect at the outset. Even the most cautious of intended victims would find it hard to resist the expert amongst us. The competent *shearer* has the ability to come across as a sort of new friend and not merely a sales person at all. This established, the 'target' makes an easier victim. If your would-be customer is in a more relaxed frame of mind, then he can be swayed, with certain exceptions, into buying. Some take longer than others, the barriers of mistrust and caution take differing times, and indeed different ways to overcome, depending on the individual concerned. The vast majority had the common sense to be wary when buying a banger. I succeeded in putting most of them at ease so to speak.

To my advantage, the various forms of media, newspapers, T.V. etc, were constantly painting an evil picture of the second-hand car dealer. By far the worst type of car dealer, or so the consumer press would have you believe, is the nasty fellow selling bangers. The portrait that they paint is one of a very shady, fast talking, 'Arthur Daley' type. The last thing a punter expects is to be talking to someone, who on first impression, does not even want sell them anything at all. In fact he even puts you off buying some of them. A favourite ploy of mine was to pretend to be a mere, underpaid, over-worked, employee of the management. Who incidentally I had no love for. I then proceeded to point out the better cars on the pitch, whilst also pointing out a few 'bad' examples. I am then, in their eyes, on their side against the 'big bad owner' of the pitch. This ploy worked virtually every time, after all it must have been a very satisfying feeling knowing that you had got the better of a ruthless car dealer, aided by his un-faithful employee. Quite the reverse was the truth of course. I have always said that a good salesman would make a very capable impressionist, or vice versa in fact. I wonder how some of my victims would have reacted if they had found themselves facing Mike Yarwood or maybe Les Dennis. If only punters realised, that the man they talk to regarding a prospective car purchase, is very rarely the man that they think he is. Although to the uninformed, the art of salesmanship <u>seems</u> straight forward, I can reliably inform you that the <u>good</u> sales professional is a totally different guy in real life. For instance although an outgoing personality helps the majority of sales people, I know of quite a few shy members of the profession. Shy in the respect that they put on one show for their public, but in real life are somewhat less outgoing, as are quite a few members of the show business fraternity.

Some actors for instance are of this ilk, they put on a very convincing performance to the public, but in their private lives turn out to be somewhat retiring. In a way the less forward types of salesmen must experience a lot harder task than their counterparts, as their own personality must be one of the greatest obstacles to overcome.

Enough of my wandering off the subject, I shall return to a few of the 'characters' I came across during my term of office so to speak. One of these people was a timid little man I shall call Martin. It took me all of twenty minutes to 'open him up'. He seemed extremely wary of people in general, let alone someone about to relieve him of his hard-earned cash. He was about as talkative as a radio with it's batteries missing. Obviously a by-product of the T.V. series 'That's Life'. After viewing every car on the pitch, some twenty-eight or so, twice!, he finally decided on a Mini Clubman estate, with eleven months M.O.T. remaining. It was, funnily enough, quite a decent example and an obvious bargain at the knock-down price of only £150. It came in as a part-exchange on another vehicle and so owed us practically nothing. I managed to prise the vast sum of £20 as a deposit for the said little gem. He said that he would collect his purchase later that day and off he shambled into the distance. The scruffy duffle coat that he was wearing made him look like some sort of constipated train spotter. As previously stated it was quite a nice car, even by my standards. In all truth he had obtained one of the few bargains on the yard. There was a small hole in one of the front wings and a wiper blade was missing, but apart from these the car was well worth the asking price. I turned my attention to hopefully, bigger spenders who were looking around one of my other gems, at three times the price of Martin's dream car. They obligingly bought the car, with very little of the old 'Milton magic' having to be dispensed – the whole sale from start to finish taking only ten minutes to complete. If only young Martin were so easy to please.

Later on that day I got a call – it was the constipated train spotter, "Hello it's Martin here, I'm the fellow that left you a deposit on the Mini estate." I replied in a cynical posh voice " Yes sir, it's ready for you to collect at anytime that suits you best." Martin then spurts out, "Well I've been to the Trading Standards and they say that you've got to repair that hole in the wing and fit a new wiper before I take it away."

Well to say I was fuming at this little lad's cheek was an understatement. I said in as calm a voice as I could, "Who do you think we are Martin? Bloody Kennings or something. I think you had better come down here and we'll have a word about it."

Now I must admit I've had a few punters go to the local Citizen's Advice etc, After they have driven away their purchase, but never, never had they gone to them before they had purchased a car. He had not even taken the car for a test drive for God's sake, let alone driven away in it. To say I was slightly gob-smacked, was a fair description of my amazement. Martin arrived on foot, with the hood of his duffle coat over his head this time. Well it was raining by this time – and his coat certainly needed the wash! I stood in the office doorway effectively keeping him standing out in the downpour. Trying to keep myself from grabbing him by the throat, I asked him what he thought he was doing. Being the little introvert that obviously was he whispered, as he talked down into his chest, that he only to be sure he got a good car. As he uttered these few words I am sure I could see him trembling. Containing my rage as best I could, (the cheek of the little shit, £150 and he wants it to be a sparkling gem, the likes of £2000 wouldn't buy), I said to him – roughly translated that is, "Go forth and multiply." The whispering duffle coat then asked for it's deposit back. (Brave little bugger ain't he?)

I said in a patronising tone, "Oh I can't let you have that back I'm afraid." Martin then said, as brave as he dared, "Er why not." I was unable to contain myself any further, "Because, Martin, you brave little shit, I would have to kick you all around this yard before I did that." Before I had even finished speaking our Martin was scorching a trail through the gates homeward bound. (Rotten Bastard aren't I?) I never heard from the duffle coat bedecked Martin again.

I sold the Mini estate two days later, for the same price, with no complaint from the purchaser, on the contrary he was delighted with his acquisition. It was sold with the same 'faults' and not a sign of the Trading Standards to be seen anywhere. I pity the man that eventually sold our 'fussy' Martin a car . But look on the bright side, if the vendor was a lonely man, by chance he would be well pleased, as a lad like Martin would hang around like a bad smell, bringing the car back with every little thing that went wrong. After all Martin only wants to make sure he gets a good car doesn't he ?

I will now take time out to illustrate the subtle art of telling the news 'As it is' – as portrayed by the newspapers of this country. During the winter of 1989/90 a school teacher and his equally self-pretentious wife, ambled onto the pitch. I used to get quite a number of the so-called better-off members of our society, gracing my lowly premises. They had first and foremost been attracted to the low prices I had on the screens of my 'little gems'. The act of saving it seems was not exclusive to the poorer members our nation. (Cynical bastard that I am.) I strived to price my stock competitively, as the only rival that I had to face was the private individual. This form of bait always worked, the chance of picking up a bargain was an irresistible lure. Even some of my more expensive cars were a giveaway compared to the prices of other dealers. The main difference between my cars and those of the others was, that my cars were usually bodged up heaps of scrap. I did sell a large proportion of straight cars too, but the profit was a lot more on a bodged car than a straight one. All our cars were roadworthy at least (just), as they had to be, to keep within the law,but as I have described earlier in this book, that can mean very little about the cars general condition. A good ploy I used quite often, would work like this. The average punter could not comprehend why my prices were so much cheaper than anyone else's. This set alarm bells ringing in their heads To allay all or most of these alarm signals certain 'obvious signs' were left un-repaired on some cars. If the real reason for the cars cheapness was because it had a knackered engine, or clutch or whatever.

The punter would, after an adequate bodge, have no reason to suspect anything amiss. Especially if the bodywork was tarted up. His natural reaction would be to think, 'at this price it looks too good to be true, there must be something wrong with it'. The punter would then do one of two things either: (a) give the vehicle a lot closer inspection than was considered 'normal' and consequently find (if mechanically minded enough) the far greater offending fault. Or (b) bring down his 'solicitor', (a term we use for an independent mechanic, the usual phrase was, 'Oh no he's brought his solicitor with him'.) to give the car a thorough examination. Any bodged car would subsequently, in most cases, be exposed.

But most car sales of such vehicles could be achieved by leaving faults like scruffy bodywork, a few bald tyres, etc, to give the punter the impression that, the only faults on the car were the ones he could see, and therefore the reason for it's apparent cheapness. Most average punters would think to themself 'ah these bits could be done pretty cheaply, and at this price it's a bargain' or something along such lines. To help to think along these lines I would select a speech from my repertoire, improvised to suit every particular punter, but took the form of: 'Why go round the corner and pay their prices, because all you are doing is buying a car in the same state as this' I point to the car in question. 'That has been tarted and bodged, and lord knows what is under all that paint. At least when you buy one of ours you can see what you're buying, (by this I mean the few bits that have purposely been left untouched) before you start to sort it out. We don't do anything to any of our cars, prior to you buying them, and so you see them with all their warts, so that you know what you are getting. After all the other dealers buy their cars in worse state then these, they just bodge them up, and within a few weeks the flash car you paid all that money for, ends up in the state it was in, in the first place. The only difference between those cars and this one is that you will pay up to <u>double</u> for one of their cars, which will end up looking worse more often than not than this one looks now. When you buy a car from us your know what you are getting right from the start, and the saving you make is a lot more than you would pay to have those little jobs sorted out <u>properly</u>. Why put money in the pockets of dealers like that, when you can do the sensible thing and save the money for yourself?'

I then give them two final points of sale, that usually close the deal, 'all we do when you buy our cars is to make sure that they run O.K.. We leave the little bits, put a little bit of profit on top of the price we paid for them, and then we sell them. All we want is, if at the end of the week we can make ourselves a wage, then we're satisfied. We don't want to sit back smoking big cigars and driving a flash car, we just want to earn a living, hence our low prices'. The second and most effective statement I impart is this, 'if you're worried about repairs, don't be. Lets face it, it's not so much what you initially pay for a car that matters, it's what you may end up paying to keep it on the road that really costs. No problem when you buy a car from us, we pay our mechanic £30 per day. If ever you need any repairs done to any car you buy from us, (while ever you own the car), just give us a call and book it in. All you have to do is throw him the parts, and pay his wage for the day it's as simple as that.

We don't want you breaking down, and then telling everyone what rotten swines we were selling you a dud. We want you out there driving around – because whilst you're mobile and running, you're hopefully, telling other people how much of a bargain you bought and how your repairs cost you nothing. Whilst other car owners are having to pay high street prices, you just pay, £15 a half day, or £30 a full day, not £30 an hour like some of the big dealers charge for labour. Our mechanic will also fit second hand parts if you wish – to keep the cost of any repair even lower, he doesn't insist on fitting brand new, as the high street garages do. We want you, on the road, telling your friends how good we are to our customers. Word of mouth is, we have found, one of the best and cheapest forms of advertising. You won't find a better deal, on a cheap car, anywhere. We look after you. If you say to a private man, "Now that I've bought your car will you do me cheap repairs while I own the car". When he's finished laughing I think he'll say no. It's a very difficult thing to portray the exact manner and approach that a sales pitch is given, but I can assure you, the previous piece of 'verbal engineering' nine times out of ten secure the sale. For the odd one or two that still was dubious and were thinking of trying the private vendor or maybe a few, I had this snippet to add, "Well you may get a slightly better looking car from out of the classifieds, but will you get peace of mind. The first time your car has a major breakdown I bet you say, I wish I'd have gone to Bill's Bangers". At least if you have any problems with any of our cars it won't cost an arm and a leg to have it put right. Let's be realistic, all cars breakdown at sometime or other, and I think if common sense prevails, you'll end up making the right decision. They more often than not <u>did</u> make the right choice. (Or maybe not if you think about it.)

As for this load of tripe I was telling them, about cheap repairs. If anyone did happen to phone and book a car in I always told them that at that particular moment in time we were booked up solid and I would consequently give them a date some three weeks or a month hence. This usually had the effect of putting them off, as they wanted to be on the road <u>now</u> – not in a month"s time. Our mechanic was far too busy to start messing around with past victim's cars, and besides he had to bodge more cars, to enable me to give a few more innocent punters, the same line.

Let's get back to our school teacher and his gormless-looking wife. If I thought that young Martin was a 'fussy' punter I had a lot to learn. The teacher and his wife, shall we call them Mr & Mrs Holmes, rolled up in an old Chrysler Alpine, not one of the greatest cars at the best of times, but this one was so bad, I wouldn't even have given it room on my 'death row' (where I parked all the <u>really bad</u> cars, too rough to bodge). A lot could be ascertained about a punter, by observing what sort of car they turned up in, and what the state of it was. They strolled into the yard at approximately 9.30 one Friday morning. They were still 'just looking' at 11.30. I had long since left them to it, after giving them the full statement for the first hour. I was just expecting them to pull out a picnic hamper, and sit down in the middle of the yard for lunch, when, after test driving some fifteen cars, they finally showed more than a passing interest in a Ford Fiesta.

Mr Holmes' mechanical knowledge, I discovered, to be flattering, was very minimal. He was to 'fault' each car in turn for such things as, 'driving position isn't quite right' or 'Oh I don't think your mother would be able to manage the back seats', or, 'I think the seating is not quite the comfort I'm looking for'. I finally succeeded in getting him to shell out for the aforementioned Fiesta, not quite the car he was looking for, (I don't think such a car existed) but it would have to do. The price was £395, it's only major fault, (as luck would have it he had picked one of the un-doctored vehicles on the place, in short, not a bad little motor) was that someone had fitted a new wing, and it had not yet been painted to match the rest of the car, as part of the deal, I agreed to paint the wing at a later date. (He would be lucky.) He did ask if I would take his rust bucket of an Alpine in part exchange. Needless to say I pointed him in the direction of the local scrap yard.

The ultimate insult came when he decided to part with his money, he offered me a cheque. God, I thought, these middle-class types and their cheques. I explained that <u>all</u> dealers would not part with a car until he had the cash. Therefore if he insisted on paying with a cheque he would have to leave the car a few days, until the required time had elapsed for the said cheque to clear. After convincing him of the fact that cash did not bounce he sallied forth to the high street bank on foot, as his car was in no fit state to drive any further, (a captive audience no less). By 3 o'clock that afternoon he and his dear wife, who had a face on her that would fit perfectly the bottom of a frying pan, were dispatched minus £395 in crispy new notes.

Mr Holmes kindly phoned me the following morning, Saturday, announcing, "Good morning, Jeremy Holmes here, I just thought I'd phone and tell you that the car that I bought yesterday caught fire last night."

"Oh dear I hope no one was hurt," I said with genuine concern.

"No. No. I was in it on my own going for a takeaway, when I saw smoke coming from the dashboard, so I stopped the car and got out – I thought it best."

"Is the car a write off then?" I enquired.

"Well there were flames over thirty feet high so what do you think?" came the slightly cynical answer.

"Ah I see," was my comment. To which he retorted "Yes I just thought I'd let you know, that's all goodbye."

End of call, he hung up. I thought 'My he's a cool one, what does he expect me to do I wonder, give him another one to burn and see if he can reach forty feet this time?' I did feel for a fleeting moment like saying, "Well I suppose this means you won't be wanting your wing painting now?" but my sense of decorum prevented it. I heard nothing from Mr Holmes again, although I did get a number of reports of a Fiesta being burnt out in the centre of Chesterfield. On the following Tuesday I received a phone call from an enquiring reporter of the local paper. The conversation went along the following lines:

"Could I speak to the owner please."

"Yes that's me," was my swift reply.

"My name's Alan Sark, I represent the 'Derbyshire Record' I believe that you sold a Fiesta to a Mr Holmes."

"That's quite correct." I tried to sound non-committal.

"You are aware are you not, Mr er ..." (He was trying to get a name to plaster all over his rag.) I helped him finish his sentence, "That it burst into flames? Yes I am aware of that fact." I didn't give him a name, he continued, "Did you also know that since buying it from yourself, he had only driven in total seven miles."

He was hoping to provoke some form of admission of guilt or sympathetic response to this remark. Possibly hoping for me to admit that I was to blame, and that I should reimburse the poor, hard-done to, Mr Holmes. If this Mr Sark thought he could scare me into such an act, he was very much mistaken, who did he think he was? Obviously our Jeremy had been told by the Trading Standards, Citizens Advice, solicitors etc, they could do nothing for him. Therefore the 'clever' little Jeremy thought that the local press might reek revenge upon me.

Any 'normal' trader may well have shit himself over all the potential aggro and adverse publicity, but not me I <u>thrived</u> on it. In answer to his leading question therefore, I said, "No I didn't, but electrical faults, as the fire brigade can inform you, can develop without warning, even in new cars".

"You do realise that this means that the Holmes family no longer have a car and you are £395 better off." He was certainly fishing for a quoted response to this statement, and I was not going to disappoint him. After all said and done, it was not my fault that the accident happened. If it had been my responsibility I'm sure that the local Trading Standards lads would have jumped at the chance to nail me. I therefore answered the loaded question like so, "I'm very sorry to hear of Mr and Mrs Holmes' plight, but I don't see this has anything to do with me, had they not had the sense to insure the vehicle, as is the statutory requirement by the law, and anyway should be common sense?" What were the Holmes' hoping for, me to shell out, as well as the insurance company?.

"So you have no plans to reimburse them or of giving them a replacement car?" he was getting down to the nitty gritty stage now and was expecting a spur of the moment, angry response from me to be quote. I did not intend to give him any such quote, even though I didn't give a toss what he wrote. Why should I make his job easy for him? I therefore gave this response, "It's all very unfortunate for Mr and Mrs Holmes, but I'm afraid it would not be possible under the circumstances for me to comment any further. (In other words, Mr Sark, go forth and multiply.) I hung up the telephone and returned to more important matters, fleecing my flock. Pete was crapping himself over the affair, but saw the good sense in leaving it to me.

The conversation between myself and Alan Sark was broadcast to the local public, in a front page article, in the following week's edition. Complete with a photograph, taken of Mrs Holmes holding a baby, (obviously to accentuate the gravity of the situation – that could have been my baby in there), through the burnt out wreck's window. A very effective photograph indeed. I was quoted as saying everything that I did my hardest not to say. Bill's Bangers was painted, in very vague terms of course, as some sort of evil purveyor of flaming death traps. This was all aimed, with the intention of making me see the error of my ways, and give them their money back or a free car. Even if I didn't do the right thing, so to speak, as they saw it, the article was targeted – in their estimation that is, to affect my trade and reputation.

It seemed to me to be an attempt at emotional blackmail, they would be waiting a long time if they were hoping for this stance to work. Who were they trying to kid? As far as affecting my trade was concerned, it had in fact the reverse effect. I sold a record number of cars the week immediately after the article, a lot of them jokingly asked for a 'red -hot bargain'.

To show the Holmes' my contempt for their pathetic attempt at blackmail I had my weekly advertisement (which incidentally was placed with a rival local paper) altered to suit the situation that week, and it was worded like so;

BILL'S BANGERS

It's PYRO week at BILL'S
come and get your RED-HOT BARGAINS

'T' Reg Cortina in flame red, 2000GL,
T & T, Sports Wheels, Spoiler, Spots, Etc,
come on down and burn some rubber all you budding street racers at £295.

'W' Reg Fiat 127,9 months M.O.T. You'll not win any races in this, but at least The Price Is Hot at £275

'V' Reg Allegro 1300 HL, Taxed 2 months, tested 7 months, Needs a fire bomb up it's backside to make it move, but if you've a burning desire to own it the price is £250

'W' Reg Rally Prepared Escort, 2 Litre engine,
Lowered, suspension, harnesses, roll cage, RS Alloys Full Peco exhaust, etc, you name it it's got it,
including a FIRE EXTINGUISHER Price on application.

The usual crap about cars bought for cash etc, was added at the bottom. I think I had made my point though don't you?

Two weeks after the article had appeared in the 'Derbyshire Record', I received what I thought at first was a hoax phone call, but it turned out to be genuine, and the caller was a reporter from none other than, 'The Sun' daily newspaper. He asked me for a comment on the whole affair, I stated that it was just a bit of bad luck and that it could happen to anyone. He said to me, "What do you think caused it to go up in smoke?" I said that I really had no idea at all, but that it was more than likely due to an electrical fault, and that was the opinion of the local fire brigade, that being the case it was not the fault of anyone in particular. He finished his enquiry by saying, "and so really it was an act of God?" I replied, "They're your words not mine – I wouldn't quite put it like that".

The article was printed two days later, taking up a nominal two column inches on page eleven. It was headed with the words, 'Flaming Fiesta' and briefly described how the fateful Mr Holmes had purchased his £395 'banger' from a garage called Bill's Bangers and after a few miles it burst into flames. It then finished with the words, a garage spokesman said, "It was an act of God" – so much for factual quotations.

The possible cause of the fire came to light in a rumour, being bandied around a few weeks later, that Mr Holmes had fitted a stereo into the Fiesta, (in the exact spot that the fire brigade had stated the fire could have in fact started), prior to his fateful journey that evening. Taking into consideration the vast mechanical knowledge Mr Holmes possessed, I think it a good bet that the stereo, was indeed the culprit. It seems our Mr Holmes' inadequacy turned his trip to 'Kentucky Fried Fiesta'.

One small point of irony concerning the whole incident is this – at the time that Mr and Mrs Holmes bought the Fiesta, it's market value was considerably greater than the price they in fact paid. The assumption would be therefore that Mr and Mrs Holmes, could have informed their insurers of their loss, and then have been paid the market value of their car, a lot more than they had in fact initially paid for it. But as the actual price they had indeed paid for the vehicle, had been broadcast to the nation so to speak, they would only receive £395 from their insurers and not it's true market value. I satisfied myself that justice had been done – end of story.

After six months of very profitable trading, Pete made a decision, that to this day, I could never understand or see the logic in. He may have had quite sound and valid reasons, for what he did, but he certainly never confided in me as to why he had reached such a decision. The decision he made – to take in a partner. I, even though the whole place revolved around me, was merely an employee of Pete's, a very well-paid one, but nevertheless, an employee. I was therefore a little apprehensive when he announced that he had indeed decided to take on a partner. My first thoughts were of just packing it all in at this news. That would mean, without boasting, that Bill's Bangers would effectively cease to exist, and subsequently, would be taking a partner into nothing.

I was assured by Pete that my situation would not alter, indeed if the business was to carry on my situation had to remain relatively unchanged otherwise I would change the whole thing myself into nothing. I had them by the short and curlies really, but all I was concerned about was that I be allowed to run the selling side of the business, in the manner that it had been carried on previously. It was made clear to Pete that if Bill's Bangers ceased to give me pleasure in it's running, that is once it stopped being fun, I would throw the lot in and go home. I stayed on these terms unless things altered to the contrary, Bill's Bangers was still to be mine, in theory at least.

When Pete introduced his new partner, I was not exactly filled with the feeling of optimism and confidence. He was a nice enough fellow, in fact too nice. He did not seem on first impression, to be the type to take to cars like a duck to water. Basically he seemed too honest. He lacked, (unless he was hiding his light under a bushel), that 'killer instinct' so to speak. This then was my first impression of Michael Palmer. A small – on the surface anyway – happy little man. His most distinguishing feature was his nervous laugh. I came to nickname him, 'Mickey the Mouse'. All the time that we had been trading Pete kept no records or proper accounts. Mickey, whose wife was an accountant, was to try and change all this. Even with his "faults" he was a very likeable person, and therefore found myself carrying on in the same capacity as before, despite my obvious dislike for it, making my cash the 'legal way'. (In effect paying tax and National Insurance.)

Mickey never realised the full extent of the underhand dealings that were carried on within the car trade, to use his words, "Well I thought there were a few fiddles in my old job, the building game, but this business is dog-eat-dog", My reply to his statement was simple, "Yes Mickey, that's quite right, but all the rest are Yorkshire Terriers and I'm a Great Dane." Meaning not many car people, punters and dealers alike, ever got the better of yours truly. Mickey's attempts at legalising the business were about to begin. He started off on the right foot, everything was recorded, all items that were purchased he wanted a receipt for, the regular sort of thing. You know what I mean. This carry on was O.K. until one day it dawned on him to accompany our mechanic to the local scrapyard. This was probably an attempt to show our employee, that Mickey's new policy was very easy and straight forward. Lord help him!

The normal way of dealing at such places is with cash, and the odd time a little bartering may achieve the bargain that you are after, but as for the trappings of modern day living, like cheques and credit cards, forget it. This particular time, the necessary parts were duly removed from the donor vehicle concerned and Mickey paid for them in cash, as was the norm. It was the added comment that brought a puzzled expression to the scrapyard owner's face. Now old Harry, the man he was dealing with, was somewhat taken aback when Mickey uttered the words "Can I have a receipt for that mate? The number of receipts that old Harry had probably issued in his entire life could have been counted on the fingers of one hand, but more like the fingers of one finger. Harry was the size of a double decker bus, and Mickey being only knee-high to the proverbial grasshopper. Harry must have put the fear of God into poor little Mickey, when he growled back in reply to his request. "Look 'ere young 'un we've got back seats and rear seats, but I never give no f*****g re-seats, so piss off."

Needless to say Mickey did not pursue his request any further, this was just one lesson of many that our dear little Mickey was going to learn about the motor trade .

Mickey's mechanical knowledge gave rise to the saying of, "A little knowledge is a dangerous thing". I had him constantly following me around as consequence of this. He was of no use to Pete in the workshop, helping with his "projects " was a definite No - No. A lot of trade secrets were wasted on him. He quickly discovered his vocation in life though, plus it was the only thing you could trust him to do. His entire day consisted of sitting at my desk reading newspapers and magazines. I uncovered his ability, or should I say lack of it, at selling cars at a very early stage. On a scale of one-to-ten he rated as minus three. His greatest stumbling block was his natural shyness of strangers – in fact he would have made an ideal victim, certainly not a *shearer* by any stretch of the imagination .

It was not long after Mickey had joined Bill's Bangers, that we were to be subjected to another attempt by the powers that be, to achieve our downfall. Their planning was something of a farce from the offset. Their attempt might have had greater effect had they carried it out on a week-end. They could probably have cost us a couple of punters if the timing was right. Instead they chose a traditionally quiet Tuesday morning to make their move. The gates had been opened, by myself, only a matter of ten minutes, when a police van closely followed by an unmarked van and two cars, screeched to a halt across the entrance. My first impression (with tongue in cheek), was "Oh my God, we're being raided by the Sweeney! I knew that whatever they had come for, they couldn't do anything of consequence – I was too careful for that. All these dramatics were obviously aimed at worrying us to death and they had come to show us that they meant business. Pathetic!

Now if I was just your normal, easily-intimidated member of the public, of which I certainly was not, I could well have given in to their efforts. But because I was an expert at walking just this side of 'the line'. Any attempt at intimidation only succeeded in me laughing at their comical antics. Ah well, back to the convoy outside the gates. The whole lot of them were assembled in front of me, when their leader flashed an I.D. card and asked, "Could I speak to the owners please, I'm Mr Brady from the Ministry of Transport. I believe it's a Mr Day I need to speak to." Obviously he had been warned about me, and so thought he could get a better response from Pete. No such luck. Pete knew only too well how to handle such gentlemen as these, after all he had a good teacher did he not? Mickey would have been the weak link in the chain if any, but he had the good sense to keep quiet when such matters arose. Besides, I ran too tight a ship so to speak, for any major catastrophe to occur. The copper from the police van closed the gates and stood guard by them. How dramatic they try to make it all seem – f****** idiots.) The card flasher followed me to the office, from where both Mickey and Pete were watching the proceedings. When I opened the office door Mickey's face reminded me of a rat being cornered by a ferret. He was <u>shitting</u> himself. Pete was calm and collected, a prize pupil no less. Myself and Pete knew that whatever these men from the Ministry did, there was no way that they could stop us trading. The only teeth that they had, were to be sank into the backsides of M.O.T. testers and testing stations, they could only bark at us. The Ministry men were unaware of my knowledge as to the extent of their powers and limitations. Mickey didn't know either. Pete knew, or at least had a good idea that they were powerless, just by looking at my smiling face. I watched the naive little Mickey crapping himself and thought to myself, "you're in the wrong business my son". The only authority that the Ministry men possessed was over the numerous testing stations up and down the country. But they could, without warning, do exactly as they had done this particular morning, to any motor dealer although in practice it is somewhat of a rare occurrence. They were, in short, concerned with the roadworthy condition of any cars that we had for sale. Especially in relation to any faults on the said vehicles, which in their estimation could have been present at the time of the original M.O.T. test that it had been put through. In other words they were looking for 'bent tests'. They were wasting their time on my pitch, I was guilty of a lot of things bordering on the illegal, but I found no need to use 'bent tests'. They were trying their hardest not to show their true intent, but to a man like myself their aims were only too apparent. One must remember at this point, that they thought, at best they were dealing with gifted amateurs, and thought they going to show us how it was done by the professionals. The efforts of these 'professionals' – naturally, failed, and obviously resulted in a gross waste of public resources. They were just another attempt in harassing us into closing down. But they were not dealing with any Tom, Dick or Harry. I was, at the very least, their technical equal, in as far as the law permitted me to be, and in a lot of respects I was in fact better. They after all had to go by the book, I had read their book. The book of rules governing the way I played the game had after all, had yet to be written. This was not to be the last attempt at harassing us out of business, not by any means. It would certainly not be the last time that their efforts would fail either. The only 'penalty' that they managed to impose was the insistence that a Cortina that we had on sale, be fitted with two tyres before it was sold. The tyres in question were below the legal limit. After solving the problem (by swopping two tyres from another Cortina) we duly drove the car up to the local testing station, to have the little form listing the fault concerned, (left by the powerless Mr Brady) duly stamped. It was then dispatched to the 'Men from the Ministry' – end of the affair. My that <u>did</u> hurt. We were thinking of closing down as they had frightened us that much. <u>They should be so lucky</u>. The local powers that be were to try yet again to seal our fate, this time using a different department, but I shall come to that particular event later. Now to a lighter moment in the pitch's history.

It was now spring, the beginning of April, quite a fine morning with the sun just breaking through. I was feeling good and ready for anything the day had to offer, well I thought I was. An old Triumph Dolomite drew up outside the gate, crammed full of Pakistani kids, and being driven by a smartly- dressed Asian woman of around thirty or so. The kids stayed in the car, thank God. All I needed was a tribe of ankle-biters to ruin the day. Kids always seemed to treat 'Bill's Bangers' as some sort of adventure playground, and the thought of seven or eight little terrors running rampant over the pitch did not exactly fill me with glee. The woman, after screaming into the car through the driver's window, walked over to me beaming from ear to ear with what I can only describe as, a 'pretend' smile. Instead of being greeted with the expected Asian accent, she said in the broadest Sheffield I have ever heard, "Hey 'as da gor any big estates gooing chee-app?" Somewhat taken aback to hear such an accent emanating from the Asian woman's mouth, I replied, "Well I've got a couple that might fit the bill." The *shearer* in me was soon taking control, who cared what she looked or talked like, money is what mattered. That's what I was there for, to take their money. We had an old Granada estate and a Cortina estate which, even though I say it myself, was the best example of a Ford estate I had seen in a long time, to use a trade term it was 'mint'. After the usual sales patter it was obvious that, the Granada she could afford, the Cortina she could not. The prices were

£325 and £450 respectively. To say she took a liking to the Cortina would be slightly misleading, she loved it. When I ascertained that she did not have the rupees for it, I tried in vain to sell her the Granada. She was however adamant that she was having the Cortina. Her words were explicit and straight to the point, "Look darlin', I'd do anything if you'd let me have this car for £375 because that's all the money I've got in the world, and when I say anything, I mean I'd do <u>anything at all!</u>" She was winking and pouting as she said those words. I thought to myself "She's having you on mate, and even if she isn't you can't spend sex, so, no money, no car." To bring her back down to earth again I said "Look love I couldn't let you have this car at that price, no way." If I had any doubt as to what she meant by <u>anything</u> she made it abundantly clear with her next statement. "I'm very good you know, I bet you've never had an Asian woman have you? I've got to have this car, you'll not regret it, we could go in that shed over there." She was pointing to the workshop where Pete was in residence, working on his current 'project'. I had no desire to, 'go where every man has been before', and so I saved myself from her dubious charms by saying, "Well love as nice as you are, I've got take cash for this car it's against my religion not to. Anyway I only work here, I'd probably get the sack for even knocking a fiver off, never mind £75."

"Oh so you don't own all this lot then, who does own it? Can I have a word with them?" Now Pete was a 'poser' who fancied himself with the girls, and so I thought "Right let's see what the bugger can do with her, I could do with a laugh." I pointed at the workshop and said, "Go in there and ask the guy who's welding, his name is Pete, he owns the place."

Off she swaggered to the workshop to try her Mae West impression on the totally unaware Mr Day. She had been in the workshop only three minutes, when Pete came tearing out. "How much is that Cortina estate Alan?" After telling him the price I had got it up at, he said in an almost begging voice, "Do you mind if I let this bird have it for a bit less, only she's stripped off on the back seat begging for it, go on, I'll make it up to Mickey for his share." Mickey was out, trying for more re-seats I suppose . I didn't have the heart to tell Pete no, "Look if you're sure, square it with Mickey, go ahead, you must be mad." There were some weird noises coming from that workshop during the ensuing twenty minutes, and they sure as hell weren't mechanical ones, more like farmyard impressions if you ask me. Pete came into the office beaming and said, "She says if we knock the price down to £300 you can go in and get your share." I replied, "No thanks" the price was low enough at £375, and my financial instincts took precedence over animal urges any day. besides imagine having to tell Mickey that I let a car go for £150 less than it's possible price, just because she was good to the lads . "Anyway we'd have a right job explaining to Mickey the reason why we didn't ask her for a receipt" I said with a laugh. Pete did the honours and sent her on her way with the Cortina estate, less £75 for her services to, the by now euphoric Mr Day. He asked me to say nothing to Mickey, as Mickey was one of these types who told everything to his wife. As she was very friendly with Pete's live-in girlfriend at the time, he felt discretion the better part of valour, I said nothing. Not that it mattered much as Pete was to split with his girlfriend not twenty-four hours later. Pete's morning exercises were to be rewarded about two weeks after his 'discount deal', when he found himself trotting along to the S.T.D.C. (Sexually Transmitted Diseases Clinic) for a generous helping of antibiotics. I somehow think he wouldn't be willing to give any more discounts to the fairer sex. It couldn't have happened to a nicer chap. I sometimes wonder about whether or not Mickey would have taken advantage of the Asian lady's offer had he been there at the time. If indeed he had, and from what I knew of the little guy, I tend to think he may well have done, what would his wife have thought, if she had found out? Even more to the point, what choice words would she have used when her doctor diagnosed that she had contracted a dose? All I can say is, that it was certainly not a dull place to work, everybody and everything was bound to be fun at 'Bill's Bangers'.

Not long after Pete's 'Asian project', he announced that he had decided to leave, and straight away at that! He gave no reason for his sudden desire to dissolve the partnership with Mickey, and his urgency was such that he was quite willing to take his leave, and ask no financial recompense for leaving his share of the business to Mickey. Extensive enquiries, and various sources of information, revealed a couple of possible reasons for Mr Day's hasty exit. By far the worst of these two was one I should certainly not wish to endure, and the way that I had conducted my car selling affairs, not likely to, thank God. Apparently one of Pete's old customers, from sunny Lincoln, a very displeased one by all accounts, had traced him to Chesterfield. Possibly this process was assisted by his ex-girlfriend, who just by chance now resided at, yes you've got it – Lincoln! This certain 'gentleman' – and I use this term very loosely indeed – was not a man to take his grievances through the normal processes of the law, and that was putting it mildly. My what a little nuisance Pete had made of himself before our acquaintance. He never did divulge his reason for returning from his adopted county Lincolnshire. (He was native to Chesterfield.) The gentleman's name was Sam Cutts, and he was more of the 'vigilante' type of fellow really. He liked to keep things more on a personal level. Mr Cutts had something of a colourful reputation, or so I am told, in the said district of Lincolnshire. It was definitely not for flower arranging, I can assure you of that. One story of his exploits imparted to me, concerned a builder in the town of Louth. Mr Cutts had cause to remonstrate with the aforementioned, something to do with his wife or similar. Sam, (I use his first name as I felt I know him so well. Ha ha!) After quite a lengthy pursuit, he had his adversary cornered in an alley. The alley was blocked off, halting the builder's retreat, by a wall some three feet in height, with a chain link fence growing vertically out of it for a further six feet – a somewhat impossible structure for the fleeing man to overcome. His victim thus trapped, Sam set about the task of re-arranging his features slightly, no not slightly, Greatly would be nearer the mark. The now face down, prostrate, well-beaten guy, was attempting to raise himself to his feet. He was hoping to achieve this by placing his hands on the top of the wall and trying to lift himself upright. Sam meanwhile, noticed a length of four by two timber some four feet in all, he picked it up. Then with the force of a steam hammer, brought the edge of the improvised club, across his victim's hands. Which were after all placed conveniently on the top of the wall. Three of the fingers were completely severed as a result. The ice-cool Sam dropped his club and picked up the screaming builder's three sliced-off digits. Then he growled these words as he shoved them into the poor man's top pocket like some fancy handkerchief, "You'd better get yourself off to the hospital pal, I hear they can do wonders with a needle and thread nowadays." Mr Cutts then left his, by now sobbing, adversary, to make his own way to the casualty department of the nearest hospital.

This then was the 'gentleman' who was hoping to have a 'word' with 'poser Pete'. One can't really blame him for wanting to decline a conversation with his old friend Sam, can you? I don't think his 'poser' image would impress, sporting a fake 'Rolex' but minus his fingers. I was sorry to see him leave really, things wouldn't be quite the same without him. I can hear a few of you saying, "What about the Police?" Well in ordinary circumstances one would feel safe in the knowledge that if Sam Cutts did catch up with Pete, he would suffer the consequences of the law But trying to tell a man recently deprived of the luxury of being able to pick his own nose with his favourite finger, that the culprit would soon be brought to justice, and that he would then be safe from further attacks, was a little in the same vein as, shutting the stable door after the horse has bolted. The police were not kindly disposed to offer protection to the likes of Pete, (a fleecer of innocent members of the public, and so, in their eyes, something of a low-life). In short until Pete received his spanking, the police were powerless, or maybe reluctant to act. The police were aware of Sam's reputation and who could blame them for not being too willing to aid who they perceive to be, a non-conforming member of society – Pete!

The second reason for his feet wanting to tread new earth, was concerning, H.M. Inspector of Taxes, and we <u>all</u> know this particular 'gentleman' don't we? Needless to say, the urge in Pete to vacate the vicinity must have been overwhelming to say the least. After all, the alternatives didn't look at all appealing .

I was left then, to the fate of having to make a car dealer out of, 'Mickey the Mouse' – no easy task. I shall be only too glad to enlighten you as to how formidable this job was to be. As I have explained briefly, previously, Mickey was shy, green, uprightly honest man. This was to be one of my greatest challenges to date, and I would not be at all surprised if I failed in the venture. The most difficult task at hand was to rid Mickey of his <u>honest</u> attitude to trading. This was an easier job than it first would seem, because our Mickey was the biggest <u>miser</u> in all the western world. Far from the accepted objective of making money, Mickey was <u>obsessed</u> with <u>saving</u> money. In point of fact, although you may find this hard to believe, he wasted more money in his attempts to, <u>save</u> a quid, than ever he could hope to conserve by doing nothing – confused? – you won't be.

CHAPTER 5

Mickey Palmer's favourite pursuit, it always seemed, was running out of petrol. Whenever it was time for him to trot off home, he would always take a car from amongst the ones I had on sale. His philosophy in this method of returning home, was that he would not have to buy any petrol, which in Mickey's eyes was a great saving. In his words, "I'll use up the oceans of petrol already in any of the cars that come in, we're not giving all that petrol away." <u>All that petrol</u> was in reality a very small amount, but Mickey's theory was, that even when a car's fuel gauge registered empty there would be plenty of petrol left in the tank. This he assumed, as a car of his some years previously had a faulty fuel gauge, so naturally it must be the same for all other cars. Such was the level of Mickey's expertise in the car trade. Needless to say on his homeward journey, a distance of some five miles or so, he would frequently run out of petrol . He <u>never</u> had the good sense to take petrol can with him when embarking upon his homeward voyage. He had to therefore, when he subsequently ran out of fuel, walk to the nearest filling station. He then was forced to purchase a petrol can, (the garages along his route had long since grown tired of loaning him one, and were in fact making a tidy sum selling him a can every time), and enough petrol to get him home. He would never buy more than the minimum amount he estimated could get him home and back to work the following day. Consequently he ran out of petrol coming to work the next day on a number of occasions, due solely to his miserly tendencies the night before. It was a very rare occurrence that he made it both home and back on the contents of any petrol tank. No amount of pleading or advice was heeded by the 'thick little miser'. This 'practice' also created some even more annoying side-effects. I lost count of the number of times that he flattened a car's battery by trying to re-start the car when he had replenished, though somewhat sparingly, the contents of the fuel tank. Often this flattening of the battery would mean he was unable to re-start the car, and so he ended up deserting the vehicle and finishing the journey on foot. As the batteries on our stock of bangers were not too good anyway, this became a prevalent problem. Our enterprising and clever owner soon hit upon a novel idea to avoid him having to endure this impromptu form of exercise. He would set off home an hour before our mechanic was due to end his shift, then, if Mickey did break down, he could phone for assistance. Our mechanic spent the last hour of most working days chasing after the stupid Mickey. I virtually begged the little shit to put a mere pound's worth of petrol into any car he took home, therefore avoiding a breakdown, and the cost recovering, both himself, and the vehicle. I might as well been talking to myself, for all the good it did. To save a pound, he would risk the journey. The cost of which, when and if he ran out of petrol, was to prove far greater than any saving he hoped to achieve. I once collected fifteen brand new petrol cans from around the pitch, all products of the stubborn little cretin's folly. After threats from yours truly, of my impending resignation over the whole affair, such was the frequency of his antics, he did, for a short while, take my advice and pay for his fuel in the conventional manner. He must have carried on the easy method of returning home for all of seven days, when he hit upon a cheaper way to obtain his fuel. This entailed him siphoning even the tiniest of fuel contents from my stock of cars for sale. The result of this was that when punters test drove a car, they invariably ran out of petrol, and in some cases would just abandon the vehicle where it was, all thanks to the penny-pinching tricks of Mr Palmer. It did reduce the number of breakdowns by Mickey himself, but it was far more maddening having to rescue potential customers. Mickey was not the slightest bit interested in my troubles – he had cured his problem after all, and was extremely proud of his achievement and a 'saving' to boot. I put all this behaviour down to one thing, Mickey was nothing but a <u>great big kid</u>. My constant complaints therefore fell upon deaf ears, as did anything carrying an adult tone to it.

I had cause to smile one day though, it was when Mickey received a phone call from his wife, who was stranded, due to a train strike, in Sheffield. Mickey selected a Granada from the front line, and estimated that the contents of the petrol tank were sufficient to carry out his 'mercy mission'. He came into the office to ask for a petrol can, just in case. It seemed he had learned something from his previous experiences. (A <u>very</u> quick learner don't you think?)

For if he was to end up stranded, his overbearing wife would certainly have something to say about his miserly ways. (She wore the trousers in their family, and made sure that Mickey didn't forget it.) I said that all the petrol cans were in the workshop. Off Mickey went to fish one out. He returned to the office with a grin on his face saying, "I've found one that's nearly full, has Bill been trying to siphon petrol behind my back?" I said it was probably for cleaning something or other and that it was only him that was miserly enough to go around the pitch siphoning. With a satisfied smile on his face he set off on his quest, happy with the thought that he did not have to spend any of his precious cash on petrol for the trip. Being the miser that he was he placed the can complete with it's contents in the boot of the Granada. If he could complete the journey without using it he would be able to save it for another day. These were the actions don't forget, of a man who was receiving something like £1500 net profit per week due to my efforts. The lunatic was scrimping and saving every last penny. His excuse for this behaviour was that he was not making anything at all, and so had to economise, who did he think he was fooling?

It was time to close up. Mickey had been gone approximately forty minutes. I was locking my office when Bill, our mechanic at the time came towards me intending to ask me for instructions for the next day. I asked him, "What on earth did you leave that can of petrol lying around for, Mickey's found it now", and presuming he had indeed siphoned it for his own car I added, "you should have put it out of sight, Mickey's used it for himself'. I thought better luck next time Bill.

I was momentarily confused when Bill replied, "and what petrol might that be?" Now he was a lot of things but he was no liar and so I said, "so you haven't siphoned any petrol today?". "No I ain't left the workshop all day". In fact I hadn't seen him on the pitch all day and so I tended to believe him. I enquired, "Well what was in that petrol can that Mickey was swanking about?"

Bill returned to the workshop and checked, when he emerged from the place his face bore a grin that a 'Cheshire Cat' would be proud of, and blurted out, "it must be that anti-freeze mixture that I drained out of the Cavalier in the workshop, it was the only sort of container I could find, out of all those cans he had to pick that one. I hope he don't end up putting that stuff in a cars tank".

We both ended up setting off home laughing our heads off at the thought of Mickey and his ever-so-posh missus stranded in the back of beyond in the pouring rain. The next morning the sad truth came to light, Mickey had indeed ended up pouring what he thought to be petrol into the Granada, and succeeded in flattening the battery to boot. He was unable to contact me as I was out for the night (or so he was informed when he rang). He had to call out a breakdown truck from a rival garage, if this was not in itself humiliating enough, it was nothing compared with the dressing down Mrs Palmer administered whilst the car was being winched up. I was not to witness the 'pipe and can' routine on the pitch again, Mickey had learned a lesson regarding the <u>saving of money</u>, he would remember for quite a while – or so I thought.

Any <u>normal</u> person one could credit with the ability to learn by one's mistakes, however Mickey, was by no stretch of the imagination a <u>normal</u> person. Even though he was in his thirties, there was no other way to describe his emotional development than by calling him a <u>child</u>. He had all the physical attributes of a man, but his actions, thoughts, moods and desires, seemed to be more and more indicative of him being a <u>child</u> trapped in an <u>adult</u> body.

He was to be allowed to carry out his childish fantasies as long as my patience permitted. For the very moment that I eventually 'threw in the towel' and left, would mean that Bill's Bangers would cease to exist.

My attempts at training Mickey were all in vain. All he seemed to be interested in was the 'glamour' of being a car dealer. His knowledge of the car trade was nil, even after six months at Bill's Bangers. Mickey thought that the owner of such an establishment, by now very well known in the local area, would hold some sort of superior standing, if not admiration in the community. This then was the main claim to fame that Mickey had, the fact that he owned the place. In no way did he contribute to it's success, indeed it was a success, in spite of him, not because of him. But he gained the greatest pleasure, from telling everyone who would listen, that he was the notorious Bill's Bangers that everyone was talking about. Whenever the majority of people discovered the author of the witty advertisements in the local press, (me in reality not the pathetic Mickey) much praise and admiration was steeped upon him. Mickey revelled in this type of situation, it made him appear to be just the opposite of his true self (a hen-pecked mouse).

His bragging and blowing of his own trumpet gave him the feeling of being someone of importance. (In fact the reverse was true, as he was completely useless as a car dealer.) Inside his tiny little head he saw himself as some sort of success. His actual definition of success would be if he could get through a day without spending money. It was whilst he was riding high on one of his ego trips that Mickey's bragging was to reap it's reward. Now I personally never informed anyone, who didn't already know that is, what I did for a living or where I worked, as a matter of fact I was very reluctant to even divulge my name – for obvious reasons of avoiding confrontation in private life with irate *screamers* or their counterparts. I was always careful to keep a low profile in strange company, after all you never knew who you might be talking to.

Mickey being the really popular outgoing sort of guy (who am I trying to kid?) was a poor holder of his liquor.

It was a Saturday night and he was just beginning to reach the stage of 'being merry'. His tongue would become a lot more flexible, after being dosed with the required amount of lubricant. He was in the process of 'glory grabbing' by giving some poor individual his rendition of how he was the clever fellow behind the famous Bill's

Bangers, when he received a tap on the shoulder from a guy of gargantuan proportions. This guy had been fleeced by yours truly some three weeks before. He had no complaint about the eventual car that I sold him, his 'beef' was with the owner of Bill's Bangers. To secure the sale I had given him the story of me being the downtrodden employee. The fellow took the story to heart apparently, and pledged that if ever he was to encounter the 'boss' he would teach him a lesson. (Mickey was off on one of his jaunts that day.) I being the poor down-to-earth, underpaid, and honest as the day-is-long, man that I was, he made up his mind to do me a favour, and reek vengeance upon Mickey on my behalf. (And no wonder, the cheek of Mickey, expecting me to sell heaps of junk, to such a nice lad as that, a good job I was on the customer's side, and sold him one of the good cars instead just so as I could get my own back on my dishonest boss.) Anyway to cut a long story short – Mickey received his just deserts that night as he sustained a mild spanking from the half cut giant – oh dear.

I think Mickey would have been slightly reluctant to even own up to being a punter of Bill's Bangers, let alone the owner, from then on – especially if all his boasting resulted in other such rewards.

I denied all knowledge of such a punter of course. The moral of this tale must be; it's one thing to rob the public, but quite another thing to rub their noses in it by boasting of the fact. I said that he should be thankful that he was getting money for nothing, which indeed he was. I left him with this thought. (I left the office to attend some punters, and tell them about my wicked boss.) If someone picked your pocket, and you later heard them bragging about it, would you take offence. Case dismissed as they say in court.

I now come to a string of events which will serve to illuminate to the full, the total stupidity of 'Mickey the Mouse'.

This tale shows primarily, the sheer childishness of our Mr Palmer to great effect, it should also portray his complete lack of common-sense. (as if such a fact were not self-evident to you by now that is). Mickey was to first of all display, his before undisclosed, 'talents' as a car buyer, to myself. It happened one sunny afternoon in August, Mickey, as was his habit by this time, had been out 'driving around' (doing nothing at all, roughly translated), most of the day. When I chanced to glance out through the office window, and saw the worst example of a Triumph Spitfire I had ever had cause to set my eyes upon, driving into the yard. (Or should I say chugging into the yard as that would be a more fitting description.) On closer examination I perceived that the driver was none other than our wandering employer. My first thoughts were, I hope he's only borrowed that thing, with fingers crossed, not bleeding well bought the wreck. Upon questioning the proud, grinning, simpleton, my worst fears were realised, he announced that he had indeed bought it, for the outrageous sum of £450. Obviously someone of the same calibre as myself had sold the heap of scrap to this 'knob head'. He was not to be deterred from his belief that he had purchased the 'Car of the Year'. My blood pressure was high enough to form a fountain when he said these words, "Bill can spend a couple of weeks doing it up for me, you'll be able to manage without him, you'll just have to roll up your sleeves and get some work done on the cars yourself".

My first reaction was, to put it mildly, one of extreme annoyance at

a) him buying the heap because the cash to pay for it was to come out of the cash I had for replacing sold stock, in effect taking cash equivalent of four cars.

b) his absolute cheek at the suggestion I do some work on the cars.

I was the main contributor of work on the whole place already, and what was Mickey the Mouse going to donate in the way of labour? The usual 'sod all'. My patience stretched to the limit, but I contained my anger long enough to realise that if I finished now, poor Bill – who had only just that morning, asked me for an advance on his wages – would be out of a job. I therefore bit my lip and consoled myself with the thought that this was going to be the very <u>last time</u> that I would give in to his childish behaviour.

Quite apart from anything else, the gullibility of Mickey was becoming common knowledge throughout the trade, as the purchaser of this heap of junk, Mickey called a car, illustrated. Some clever sod of a salesman would be laughing his socks off over the sale of this one. It gave even more significance to the comedy of the situation as there was no doubt that Mickey would have made it abundantly clear who he was, and that alone would have been enough to pride himself on, managing to palm off a heap of scrap on Bill's Bangers. It was certain that the lucky vendor knew who he was selling it to, as Mickey never missed an opportunity to inform people that he was indeed the great, Bill's Bangers, I was not about to die of shame however as most members of the local motor trade knew my reputation only too well.

When I first opened up the pitch in 1989 certain of these traders estimated that I would only manage to remain open for a few weeks, how wrong they were. There were a few of the said members, after noticing that I indeed was making a success of the venture, who were asking my advice on how to get away with certain practices. One such dealer at the time of my opening had ceased to sell complete cars and had resigned himself to selling just parts. This was solely due to aggro he had received from screamers, after seeking my advice upon various aspects, he resumed car sales, and is making a very good, legal, living at it once more. I don't seek praise from such assistance, I am only to willing to help both dealer and private punter alike, so long as it doesn't affect my own trade that is. Anyway, back to the purchase of the 'amazing' Triumph Spitfire. The amount of work required to bring it back to it's former glory, was to say the least, going to cost an arm and a leg. After a 'chat' with Mickey, and his subsequent realisation that the 'thing' was indeed the wreck of the century, his stubbornness resulted in him shelling out from his own money for the heap. Just to prove that he 'knew a lot more about cars than I gave him credit for' he would renovate the car at his own expense, and in his own time, with his own hands. (My, this would prove an education.) What he should have done at this stage, was to have admitted his mistake in buying the car and chalk it up to experience, but his childish pride would not allow him to do this, instead he was going to throw more money into the futile 'project'. The car had the following faults;

    1) The bodywork was virtually non-existent, although at first glance it was hard to tell as the whole car had been 'painted' in

black underseal (using a yard brush, by the look of it) and looked an absolute mess.

2) The engine was completely knackered, belching out smoke, knocking and miss-firing.

3) There was no M.O.T. on the vehicle and on just a casual inspection, looked in no fit state to pass one, let alone on closer inspection.

In short a ten year old could have spent £450 more wisely than Mickey. The greatest offender as far as bodywork was concerned was the bonnet, or should I say lack of it. After endless phone calls and searching through motoring publications, mostly in vain, he found a supplier with a bonnet for the 'nail'. (A trade term for a wreck.) He was far too miserly to pay for a new steel replacement, and a used one was an impossibility to find, and so he opted for a fibreglass replacement. If the car was to be worth anything at all, when restoration was complete, it was advisable to use new steel panels, and not cheap plastic replacements I advised him. I might as well have been talking to a ten year old. If restoration was carried out properly he might have salvaged some of his expense when it was finished, and subsequently sold. But no, our Mickey was intending to 'pose' in the little gem, when all the work was done, he had no intention to sell it (for profit or otherwise). Therefore the more money he could save attempting the restoration of the heap the better off he would be, such was the theory in his head.

The fibreglass bonnet was duly ordered by his nibbs from a place in Gloucestershire some 200 miles away. He was going to save something like £70 on the cost of a steel one by this move, <u>or was he</u>?

When he was told by the firm that he would be waiting three days for delivery, his childish impatience prompted him to say that he would collect it personally. Apparently they would have dispatched it by Roadline, once they had constructed it.

Bill was just driving a Chevette estate onto the front line of cars for sale, as Mickey hung up the phone. He pointed to the car and said impulsively, "I'll take that estate and fetch my bonnet". I had learned through experience and past dealings with our Mr Palmer that to raise an objection was futile and so I said nothing in response to his declaration.

Without checking any levels (eg; oil, water, etc) he drove off out of the yard, with the aforementioned car to collect his precious Spitfire bonnet. The irony of the thing was, that the bonnet would not have fitted inside the car anyway. He left in such a state of excitement and haste that I didn't get the chance to inform him of this detail, not that I would have done anyway. Now when you drive any distance in a banger without first making any pre-journey checks, the odds are that you will live to regret such behaviour. Mickey's trip was no exception. After overheating – due to a slight leak from a loose hose, the car seized. Any normal driver would have noticed the temperature gauge rise and pulled up to check the engine, but Mickey was not a normal driver (in fact I can't think of anything that he does normally), he must therefore have chosen to ignore the information that the gauge was trying to give him. I tend to subscribe to the view that, such was the childish excitement and impatience of our employer that he did not even see the gauge let alone translate it's reading into the need to stop and investigate it's cause. Mickey was constantly being asked by myself, not to drive any banger at breakneck speeds, for obvious reasons, but as most children never pay heed to advice from adults, my words fell on deaf ears.

The resultant breakdown usually meant great expense, both in recovery and eventual repair of the thrashed car.

In this current case Mickey had only managed to cover fifty miles of his 200 mile trek. I refused to leave the pitch when he phoned for help at 5.30 and told him to make his way to the nearest railway station and come back by train, adding that he could recover the fated Chevette estate the following day. The next day he had to hire a recovery trailer to carry out his rescue bid. Selecting a three year old Lada from the front line he set off with the trailer in tow to recover the disabled estate. From Mickey's damage report, which was somewhat vague, the cost of repair for the stricken vehicle would not be to prohibitive, as the engine, once it had cooled down, had re-started, (well that's what Mickey had said anyway). Based upon his sketchy report I estimated that a new water pump and hose should effect an adequate repair, and then it would become a saleable item once more.

This now meant that I had two less cars to sell – even I found it difficult to sell cars that were not there. I calculated that he should return in about three to four hours. It was around 3 o'clock that afternoon before we noticed that his arrival was long overdue, he had been missing six hours with not even a phone call. He had I imagined decided to pick up his bonnet along the way, which was a childish way of carrying on but by no means out of character, taking into account his form to date.

It was 10 o'clock the following morning before I was to see his elfin features again. The story that was relayed to me was totally un-believable, and were it not for the fact that Mickey played the leading role in the whole fiasco, I would have tended to think that I was subject to a 'leg pull'. At the time that this trail of events took place, we had working for us a young lad, a general dogsbody-cum-car-cleaner. The poor overworked lad went by the name of Steve Bentley. Mickey took him along with him to recover the Chevette estate, and it was from Steve's lips that the tale was to come. (Mickey was never forthcoming with information of his stupid deeds. Mainly because he thought he had some sort of image to protect. What a joke.)

They arrived to pick up the estate and duly winched it aboard the trailer. Young Steve then presumed that they would be setting off back to the pitch. Quite the reverse was the outcome. Mickey set off for Gloucestershire towing the Chevette behind them. Such was his impatience to get his precious Spitfire bonnet. Ladas are notoriously thirsty cars, petrol economy is not high on their list of attributes. This being so one would have thought that Mickey would have the sense to return with both cars, and if the urge still too great to overcome, set off in a more economical, and suitable vehicle. Even if he did not possess the common sense to do the aforementioned, he would, giving his expertly miserly nature, leave the Chevette estate until the return journey, as his already high fuel consumption would be made even worse with another car in tow. I was, by thinking the last statement, crediting Mickey with a spark of intelligence, a vast mistake by all accounts. His frugal ways meant he was to run out of petrol a number of times during the journey. One such time was on a dual carriageway, the nearest service station was about eight miles away. You've probably guessed by now that he had no petrol can, surprise, surprise. Mickey's warped mind soon came up with a solution to his present dilemma, he would take the Chevette off it's trailer (which by chance had a towbar fitted), and replaced it with the Lada. The Chevette you remember was devoid of water, and would only run for a couple of miles or so before it was likely to seize again. Nevertheless Mickey drove the assembled Chevette, Lada and trailer set up, at his usual breakneck pace until the inevitable happened, the engine seized once more. He kept up his performance, letting the Chevette cool down and then driving it until it stopped due to overheating once again. Eventually, after two hours he got to the service station. Although by now he had rendered the engine of the Chevette completely useless.

After putting petrol in the Lada, and taking it off the trailer, he replaced it with the Chevette, then set off once more for the object of his desire – the bonnet.

Upon his arrival in Gloucestershire, the by now, very weary Mickey, was informed that his bonnet was not yet ready and would not be available until the following day. I only wish I could have seen his face. Mickey paid for the bonnet plus an extra £15 for it's delivery by Roadline.

The much disgruntled Mickey set off for home with the equally weary young Steve. For those of you now thinking this to be the end of the tale, you could not be more wrong, alas this was only to be the beginning. Somewhere along the way homeward the Lada sustained a puncture. Normally just an annoying mishap, but the phrase, 'create a mountain out of a molehill' was to only scratch the surface as a description of what was to transpire from this particular mishap. Upon opening the boot he found the spare to be useless, and to make matters even worse there was no sign of either a jack or a wheel-brace. Because of his religious beliefs, (devout miser) he chased from his thoughts any ideas of calling upon the services of a break down firm. (A bit like a Jehovah's Witness refusing a blood transfusion really.) He therefore hit upon the idea of flagging down a passing motorist and 'borrowing' their jack and wheel-brace, (all presuming that they would fit). After numerous failures he did eventually manage to stop someone – a young lad driving a Mini. The Mini, it turned out was also devoid of the aforementioned tools, and so he was sent on his way, without even the 'semblance' of a 'Thanks anyway'. He was getting a little 'cheesed off' by the time he finally did manage to stop a suitable provider of the necessary equipment. After removing the offending wheel and tyre, he replaced it with the useless spare, he then returned the borrowed jack and wheel brace to the 'donor', this time growling a very reluctant thanks, his 'charm' succeeded in getting them a lift to the local garage. His religion again raised it's head when it seemed that the ideal solution was to replace the almost bald tyre with a new one. Now Mickey's position in this religious order must have been nothing less than archbishop, and so he refused point blank to shell out the sum required for an inexpensive remould, insisting that the tyre be repaired, a much cheaper, though foolish, alternative. The repair was carried out, but he was advised to drive slowly as there was not much life left in the tyre. The unfortunate 'good samaritan' was then instructed by the arrogant Mickey to take them back to the stricken Lada. After Steve and Mickey got out of the 'samaritans' car he sped off without even waiting for any sign of appreciation from the charming little shit. (I wonder why?). This now left them with no means of changing the wheels once again. Mickey had to start flagging down drivers once again. Eventually he found a victim and the wheel was changed, but because of an ill fitting wheel brace he could only manage to tighten the wheel nuts just a little tighter than 'finger tight'. Ignoring the tyre fitter's advice he then set off at his usual pace, with his right foot hard to the floor.

 All went well, so to speak, until the repaired tyre punctured for a second time. Mickey's stupidity was to slip into overdrive this time, he completely ignored the puncture, with the steering wheel virtually wrenching itself from his hands he carried on, on the flat tyre regardless. That is until his under-tightened wheel nuts decided to part company from the wheel, no doubt due to the excessive vibration from the flat tyre. Of course the wheel eventually came adrift and the lunatic had to stop. They were on a stretch of duel carriageway about seventeen miles from home by now the time was 7.30pm. Mickey told Steve to remain in the car whilst he himself got out to inspect the damage. The wheel was nowhere to be seen, and the battle weary car was resting on the front brake disc. Any normal lunatic, if there is such a thing as a normal lunatic that is, would one would have thought, called it a day by this stage.

Mickey was not a <u>normal anything</u>, let alone a lunatic, without even searching for the wayward wheel he got back in the disabled Lada. Steve asked the state of the damage, (not that he would have known the seriousness of the situation, even if Mickey had told him). Mickey announced that it was O.K. and that they would try to get to the next garage with the car as it was. Yes that's right he was intending to drive on only three wheels. With a lot of 'riding of the clutch' he managed to get the car moving – God alone knows how he managed to steer it but he managed to move the poor Lada another mile and a half before he burnt the clutch out. This was to finally stop the maniac's advance. The last one and half miles took him a full hour to achieve, this left them both sat on a bus bound for Chesterfield, thus ended the second day of the maniac's adventure.

What sort of state he must have left the tarmac in, after ploughing a furrow some one and a half miles in length, one can only guess. Mickey arrived at the pitch on the morning of what was now the third day and announced that he was taking a third car from the front line, a Morris Ital. The reason for his choice was that it possessed the all important tow bar, by now becoming the premier requirement for any car he chose. He had not telephoned the previous night to indicate his demise. I think this was mainly due to the embarrassment of the situation rather than any other more valid reason. I didn't dare ask what had become of the first two cars, let alone whether he had managed to acquire his bonnet or not.

It was 11.30 before he returned with the trailer on which was perched the fated Chevette. By this time I had questioned young Steve about the events of the previous day. I left Mickey to unload the Chevette with Steve and went for Bill from the garage, to assist me in assessing the damage. Mickey set off with the trailer and Steve, without uttering a word of explanation, to recover the crippled Lada.

The time was 2.00pm before the pitch was to be blessed with their presence once more. It took all four of us to unload the Lada which was, to put it mildly, in a very sorry state. I tried to make a joke of the situation by saying to Bill, in a tone of voice that Mickey couldn't help but hear, " I didn't watch the news last night Bill, was it the I.R.A. or the K.G.B. that claimed responsibility for blowing up the Lada then?" Mickey remained silent, it was hard to tell whether he got the punchline or not, he just got back in the Ital and drove off. We were not to see his bright little face again that day. And so ended day number three of the Spitfire Saga.

The next morning Bill and I began to assess the cost of Mickey's fruitless mission. After taking into consideration, petrol, Bill's and Steve's wages, parts, repairs etc, the cost of his attempt at collection came to the grand total of £423, as opposed to the cost by Roadline of £15. The irony of the whole episode was that, the delivery by Roadline in actuality only took two days. Mickey's attempt resulted in three days and £423 wasted, and still no bonnet. A more salient point to mention would be, did Mickey learn anything from the affair? I doubt it very much. The cost of the heap was now almost double it's original over-inflated price, and yet more money had to be spent before it even resembled the car it was supposed to be. The eventual finished car cost a little more than £2000, and did not look to be worth anywhere near half that amount. Mickey certainly did show me what he indeed <u>did</u> know about cars – <u>sod all</u>.

It was shortly after the Gloucestershire incident that the local Trading Standards tried to put us out of business yet again, this time their onslaught was in the guise of the Environmental Health Department, concerned with Health and Safety at work.

I was sat in the office on the morning in question when in walked a pimply pair of youths both about the same age (about twenty). Although young they were as keen as mustard. (They were obviously thinking that they would show their colleagues at the council how to succeed where everyone else had failed, silly boys.) They announced who they were in unison, flashing their I.D. cards as they spoke, just like a pair of private detectives, or do I mean 'dicks'? I said that the owner was not in and that they would have to deal with me, upon asking my name, the answer I gave made them somewhat apprehensive. Had my reputation been made known to them I wondered? "We would rather have a word with Mr Palmer the owner if you don't mind" one of them managed to blurt out. I bet they would. Did I detect that they were a little reluctant to deal with me or was I being paranoid. Mickey would certainly be no match for these young whizz kids that was sure. Yet these two wimps were no problem to a *shearer* like myself, I said that it was me or nothing and that they had better make their minds up quickly, as I was a very busy man. I made up my mind to have a little fun with the unsuspecting little shits.

My plan was to see how able they were in their job, and I intended to make them as angry as possible just to see what they would react like. I knew the limit of their powers, they were unaware that I knew and they certainly had no idea what they were letting themselves in for.

Saying that they would need to inspect all the areas where work was carried out, in effect the workshop, they requested that I show them around the premises. To allay (or so they thought), any suspicion by myself, that we had been singled out for inspection, they stated that they were calling on all firms in the area. What a load of tripe, I soon let them know that I had seen through their thinly-veiled pretence. We went into the workshop, where Bill was at work. Bill, being the diplomatic type, and realising that they were official, acted accordingly to them (we had long since discussed any official attempts at sabotage, and made it clear how we stood. In other words Bill was quite free to treat these types as he saw fit). One of the pimply pair asked him if the electrical installations had been checked recently. Bill said, "What the F*** are you on about pal?" "Has the wiring been tested?" pimply said. This prompted Bill to go to a light switch and switch it on and off a few times. He then said, "There you are squire I've just tested it and it works, anything else I can help you with?"

The same acne-spotted lad said in response, "Look here friend we're here to ensure that your workplace is safe our aim is to help you". "Oh I see you're here to help me are you? Well kop hold of that hammer and chisel and knock us a hole in that steel plate on the bench will you?" "I don't think you are aware of the purpose of our visit here today" announced spotty-face number two. I then interjected, "Oh yes we know full well the purpose of your visit, don't we Bill?" Reaching for a tyre lever he said, "Yes we sure do".

The crater face twins were a little worried now. Acne-face No. 1 said, "I can see we shall, er, have to make a report and call back to see Mr Palmer when he is here".

This led me to say, "Yes I think that is a very good idea sonny. Fancy that Bill, these two gents seem ever so concerned about you working in a safe environment, I hope their report won't mean they might put you out of a job". Slapping the tyre lever in the palm of his hand he growled, "I hope not 'cos I wouldn't like that at all, not at all". "Are you trying to threaten us". Stammered No. 2. "Wouldn't dream of it Chief", smiled Bill.

"Well I suppose you've got a lot of other people to see this afternoon, I'm sure, and so suggest you leave Bill here to get on with his work, whether he does it safely or otherwise, this way gentlemen". I pronounced as I shepherded them out. Assuring me that we had not heard the last of the matter, they made a hasty exit, and drove away quick smart. They were probably going to visit the other firms up and down the same street another day, or maybe they just forgot about them. (Yes and if you believe that you'll believe anything.)

You may describe the attitude that Bill and I took as rather rash behaviour. Well, not really I was streets ahead of them. The whole emphasis of their case was to make a safe workplace for our employees. The solution was quite simple really, if we had no employees then they would have no case. We were all sacked. Mickey was then to be seen as a sole trader when the Environment boys returned with their big fat report on the unsafe working environment. Mickey was sat at his desk when the time came for their return visit. The conversation went like so. (Thanks to my coaching.)

"Are you Mr Palmer" quizzed our intrepid Health Officer. "Yes that's right". Came the reply "I'm from — —". "I know where you hail from mate, and I'm afraid no one works here any longer, I sacked them all. I don't do any repairs myself, and so l don't see any reason for you being here, do you?"

This then is what Mickey told me he said. (Probably something a lot meeker in reality, but he must have got the content correct as it had the desired effect.) He had adequately relayed my instructions. (Quite a novelty for him.) Whilst we awaited the all clear by my phone at home. The call we were awaiting came at 10.30, and we were consequently trading as per normal at 11.00am, complete with Bill and young Steve. Mickey bored us all stiff with constant renditions of his (supposed) speech to the safety men. He repeated it to us at length for days afterwards. (Well, he needed a bit of glory to cheer him up after the Spitfire Saga, and so we humoured the little shit.)

But the writing was already on the wall for Mickey, his glory days as owner of 'Bill's Bangers were numbered – sadly for him my patience had not just worn thin, it had worn completely away.

CHAPTER 6

If I were to leave without any forethought, I would succeed in killing the pitch, and all connected with it – stone dead. Although I had tired of Mickey's childishness the whole concept of my own pitch was paramount in my thoughts, besides, there was the subject of Bill's continuing employment to consider. I did owe a certain amount of loyalty to him. I had, therefore a mild dilemma on my hands. Mickey had to go, that was certain. The pitch, and all it's significant detail, I decided to keep intact. I estimated that from the moment of my leaving, Mickey would only last, at best, a couple of weeks before realising his impending doom. Some of you may think this assumption a might conceited. After all, the only thing Mickey had to do, was to employ a salesman, and he could carry on more or less as before. Point of fact was, that I had been running the place for such a long time completely single-handed, that Mickey wouldn't have known how to find the toilets on the place, let alone run the whole shooting match.

Let's take the prospect of his employing a salesman. As I have always maintained, the selling of bangers is entirely different, and a lot harder form of car selling than is the conventional way. Any 'knob-head' can sell, and more importantly buy, using a trade guide as their yardstick. All the relevant trade guides available only list cars up to eight years of age, beyond that age, you are entirely dependent upon your own experience. Therefore it goes without saying that it wouldn't take many mistakes in judgement before you found yourself in serious financial difficulty. The success of a car sales devoted to selling older cars therefore, depends upon the skill, experience, knowledge, and daring of a special kind of man. (Or woman for that matter.) Don't get me wrong on this subject there were quite a few people who were very capable of making an outright success of a place like Bill's Bangers. The main stumbling block as far as Mickey was concerned, was the fact that none of those capable would be the slightest bit interested in carrying a parasite such as he was. Indeed they would probably already be undertaking a business of their own doing the same. Mickey's fate would be sealed from the moment I announced my intended departure.

I can hear a few of you out there asking yourselves the burning question, "Why does he not start up a pitch of his own, once he has left Mickey?" The answer is quite simply this – I have never felt the need to go it alone, although I have dreamt of such a venture many times over the years. When my 'religious beliefs' are taken into account the reason for my trepidation becomes obvious. For the less intelligent amongst you (pond and plant life?) I shall elaborate. A *shearer* spends the best part of his life striving to be just that, someone who fleeces money from somebody else. Therefore the thought of going 'legal' (and subsequently <u>paying</u> other people my money, e.g. tax, National Insurance, V.A.T. etc.) goes well against the grain. Even though I like to and find it quite easy to get money, I find it very hard to hold on to it once I have got it. This creates another problem, I have never found myself in possession of enough cash to start up on my own. I suppose you could call me a latter day 'Robin Hood' really, I take from those that have it, then give it to those that don't. (Meaning <u>me.</u>)

For me to 'work' I needed a completely free hand. If I had the pressure and stress of all the paperwork and administration of a 'legal' pitch it would seriously affect the most important thing that I value in the car sales game, <u>fun</u>. Yes I'm afraid that if I didn't enjoy selling cars I wouldn't even bother. I would not mind doing all the paperwork etc, on behalf of someone else, as I had been doing for Bill's Bangers, but once that task was for myself, the magic element of <u>fun</u> would, I feel vanish.

My mission was clear then, I had to find a replacement for Mickey. Once he had flown the nest it would be a relatively easy matter to install a new 'owner'. There were plenty of candidates to choose from, after all, my efforts at achieving the success of Bill's Bangers had not gone unnoticed. The governing factor was however, the eventual new owner had to be the type that would suit me. Before I was to break the news of my departure then, I had to make sure that all was waiting in the wings – or so the saying goes.

For a number of weeks prior to my departure a suitable candidate had been buying wrecks, on a regular basis from me, to re-sell to the masses. I gave him an appropriate discount of course – one had to encourage the gifted amateur, especially as he was providing us with cash and no comebacks. He bought them on the understanding that they were his, with all their faults, if any, no *screaming* would be tolerated. He was a mild-mannered type of guy, not your normal robbing, conniving, rip-off type of character at all, not unlike me really! In many ways he was an ideal *sheep* – I liked him. I decided after much deliberation, that he was to be Mickey's successor.

Carl, as was his name, was relatively new to the car game, he had recently been discharged from the Army, although, unlike quite a few ex-Army guys, he had no mechanical knowledge. I somehow took a shine to his mild-mannered ways. In short, I would be in control. I could dictate things as and when circumstances demanded. He liked the idea of being a car sales owner. I have yet to meet any motoring type that didn't. He was, as I said previously, as green as grass, but he showed a great willingness to learn. Whether or not he was capable of learning the finer points of the banger trade was yet to be seen. By far the most important attribute in his favour however, was the overwhelming fact that he had the cash.

Once Mickey's demise was achieved, it took all of six days, it only remained for me to approach the greedy owner of the pitch, Mr Lang, once more and inform him of my intentions. The usual *shearer* charm exuded and the change of ownership went ahead. In reality as soon as Mickey had vacated the yard I shot down to the ever avaricious Mr Lang and sealed a deal on a similar standing to the original one with Bill's Bangers. The only difference being that Carl was to be the new proprietor of the car sales.

The only changes to the old set-up were small, the main one being to change the name to Carl's Cars, a small concession to make him feel in control. Everyone was in no doubt who was to be in the driver's seat, regardless of the name over the gate. It took a matter of hours to commence trading as Carl's Cars, but there was one major drawback. Carl must have got a little carried away with his personal spending prior to the takeover, as we were only able to stock out to 50% of the level that I had as Bill's Bangers. I was not too concerned about this so much, as I estimated that I could build it up to a workable level within a month. It was agreed with Carl that I build up the stock before he started to take any large sums of cash for his own use. He had no option really, he either agreed or I F****d him off. The pitch was filled sooner than even I expected in the event. So we were back trading at full capacity, robbing the public <u>legally</u> once more.

It felt like a breath of fresh air, now that the Miserly Mickey the Mouse was gone. Carl, although no fool, was as they say 'Like putty in my hands'. He was especially quick to learn the rudiments of the trade, but unfortunately lacked that killer instinct, to adequately rip-off the public at large. Which I suppose was no bad thing for yours truly, as without it, he could never make a success of Carl's Cars on his own. I was assured of a job as long as I chose to stay.

The same clientele and characters were to attend, Carl's Cars as they did Bill's Bangers. I made it abundantly clear, in all our advertising that we were different in name only. I even stated quite unashamedly, in our first advertisement, that we were more fit to con them all because we had rid the firm of it's dead weight. This was obviously a thinly disguised dig at Mickey – God bless his little cotton socks!

One of the inevitable events to raise it's head was yet another amusing tale. This time it concerned the tax disc of an old Austin Maxi which was parked on 'death row'. I arrived one morning, as per usual, to open the gates. I was greeted by a police car. My first thought was that this might be yet another attempt to bring about our closure. All thoughts of this were dashed as I was confronted with a solitary Bobby, "My, they're going to have try a wee bit harder than this I thought". The lone policeman asked me if we possessed the aforementioned vehicle. As we made our way toward the office I pointed to the car in question and said "That's it there, and the state it's in it won't be going anywhere else in a hurry, in case you want buy it officer." Upon asking me if it was currently taxed I informed him that it was, that fact was probably it's greatest asset. We both turned and walked over to the badly rusted heap, it was at this precise moment that I noticed that the windscreen was devoid of it's most redeeming feature, it's tax disc. Now I am usually one of the last to praise the efforts of the law, as by now you are probably aware, but when my companion informed that they had already apprehended the culprit, I was nothing short of amazed at their speed of detection. They had succeeded in extracting a confession, owning up to the theft of, the poor old Maxi's usefulness, it's tax disc. The proud policeman then asked if he could take a short statement, I beckoned to the office and we settled ourselves inside. I then proceeded to pour much praise and admiration upon his efficiency in detecting the crime, which had not even yet been reported. (I nearly offered him a cup of tea, I was that impressed, <u>nearly.</u>) His face then broke into a broad grin, as he said, "Well I should be only too pleased to take the credit, if it were due to my efforts that we caught him, but if you take a look at this I think it will make you a little wiser."

He slid the old Maxi's tax disc across the desk towards me. Where the make of the car was filled in when it was originally issued, there was a thick line of <u>red</u> ink over the word Austin and above it, in the same <u>red</u> ink was scrawled: <u>minni</u>. It seemed pretty obvious to me and no doubt anyone else who cared to glance at the feebly forged tax disc, how detection was achieved so swiftly. I said in utter amazement, "Good God, whatever possessed the fool to use red ink, and judging by the spelling – where ever did he go to school?"

Grinning from ear to ear the PC tried to contain himself as he informed me, "Apparently it was the only pen he could find at the time, he thought it wouldn't make any difference." As to my second enquiry, relating to where he gained his education, his was that the 'master forger' was only 16 years of age and still at school. I said that, by the standard of his current literacy, he would still be at school when he was 30.

Talking of the younger generation of car enthusiasts, we were graced one day by a lad of around eighteen. He arrived by bicycle, complete with bike clips on his trouser bottoms. I was busy on his arrival, counting some poor unfortunates' hard earned cash, in the office. The cash was the proceeds of a *shearing* earlier that day. Following a very swift look around the yard, he walked over to the office and declared, " I'll have that Escort over there please." He was pointing to an old Mk 2 Escort at £200 on 'death row', it was a decent runner, but would never pass another M.O.T. this side of last Christmas. I was somewhat intrigued by his strange manner, and so I enquired, "Don't you want hear it running or have a look at it first?" "No if you say it runs O.K. I'll have it."

"Oh it does run well." I replied. I was certainly not going to look the proverbial gift-horse in the mouth. I took his cash quick as a flash, in return I gave him the keys, log book and test certificate. Obviously it was this twerp's turn to use the family brain cell, and must have thought buying a car to be similar to purchasing a loaf of bread. I didn't care, as I have said in the past, prejudiced I am not, his cash would spend the same as the next man's. I went back to my counting, he went over to familiarise himself with his new acquisition. It was not many minutes before he came back to the office, " Excuse me, but could I borrow a spanner, to take the front wheel off of my bike, so that I can get it into the car." I pointed him in the direction of the workshop, telling him to ask for Bill. Five minutes later the Escort, complete with the dismantled bike on the back seat, crawled out of the yard at a veritable snail's pace. The 'bread man' had obviously not gained a lot of driving experience prior to his purchase. I thought this the end to the somewhat weird transaction but, as per usual, I was to discover differently

It was some three or four days later that I was to receive a phone call relating to the aforementioned cyclist-cum-rally-driver, (Joke, get it? Oh well!) The guy at the other end was the manager of a local night club. The tale transpired like so: the cyclist, up until the evening prior to his car purchase, worked as a barman, along with his girlfriend, at the said night club.

Our errant barman had ambition, indeed so much ambition, that he took it upon himself to relieve the night club of some £2000 in cash, The evening of his unannounced resignation (well, he didn't need his job now that he had come into a bit of money did he?) The cash quite foolishly had been left on a desk in the manager's office, all our enterprising young barman did was to take it upon himself to liberate the said cash, and use it to benefit the less well off. (Himself). Because of the embarrassing nature of the incident, and attempting to keep his lack of security as secret as possible, the red-faced manager took it upon himself to obtain it's recovery by other means than is the norm (Police). After interviewing the lad's girlfriend, he ascertained that, before his departure, he told his girlfriend that he would call her later, at home, with news of his plans. His girlfriend, for want of a better phrase, was something of a good time girl, and was known to like the good things in life – and I mean all of them. Our love-struck barman thought, quite wrongly as it turned out, that if he were to be well off. she would run away with him. Being the love-struck fool that he was, he phoned her as he had earlier promised, and asked the burning question, being the evil little cow that she was, she probably would have, were it not for the manager's interview some thirty minutes earlier. However she was only concerned with finding his location. (In order that the night club staff could recover the cash, and dispense a well earned spanking.) He had the good sense not to tell her his whereabouts, and said that he would call her the next day at 2.00pm. (In the hope no doubt that she would change her mind.) The night club manager agreed not to involve the police if, when he called her again, the girlfriend could get him to meet her, (This she was to achieve by agreeing to go away with him.) In the meantime the enterprising young Romeo had purchased one of my 'gems' and had decided to vacate the vicinity to avoid capture. In fact he set off southbound, down the M1.

 The old Escort, although not knackered, was no motorway cruiser. By 2.00pm, the allotted time to call, he found himself pulling into a service area some 100 miles away. He duly phoned, she managed to persuade him to return and pick her up, assuring him in the process, that they would set off into the sunset together, or something along those lines anyway. He was so excited by this turn of events that he drove off back up the motorway as fast as the Escort could propel him. His urgency was that great, and his speed that fast, he subsequently found he became the victim of a police speed trap. Upon checking the usual, the all-too-alert officers noticed their quarry's unnatural state of agitation. They subjected the car to a customary search, and discovered what was left of the previous night's takings, shoved into a pair of his sweaty socks. (Was this to try and put them off the scent I wonder?) He was duly arrested. This incident then, was to thwart any attempt at administering any form of 'rough justice' by the night club manager, a good thing for our intrepid cyclist that the police caught him first.

The reason for the phone call to me, so the manager said, was to ascertain the value of the car, which was impounded by the police at Leicester – where he was stopped. In the hope that it was worth a lot more than I had sold it him for. When he had bought it he had not asked for any receipt, and of course I didn't offer him one. The police, not noted for proffering detailed information before any case comes to court, only informed the manager that he had purchased a car from us with some of the money, but not how much he had in fact paid for the said vehicle. In the cold light of day it was discovered that the lovesick lad had managed to blow some £900 of the original cash before his eventual arrest on the northbound carriageway of the M1. I was not able to offer much relief to the night club manager's attempts at recouping the missing cash. Especially after telling him that the car, which I had sold to the 'bread man' remember for £200, was not worth much more than scrap. If it had indeed been worth something maybe the car could have been sold in order to gain some recompense. Shame really, he seemed such a nice lad to me, maybe it was the bike clips, you don't expect a guy who wears them to be such an impetuous thieving, little sod, do you? It just goes to show, you can't trust anybody nowadays. People can't all be as honest as me I suppose, ah well.

With MK2 Escorts in mind it brings me to a deal which, at the time, seemed quite spectacular – by Carl's Cars standards anyway. I had just waved off another 'plant life' in 'the bargain of the century' once more, when a convoy of very expensive cars came to a halt outside the gates. Car number one was a bright red Lotus Elite, car number two was a Porsche Carerra 911 Turbo in blue, and the third and last car in the convoy was a Mercedes 450 SLC convertible with silver coach work. No, they were not destined for my front line, as a lot of you may think, (well I can dream can't I?). Out of the Mercedes emerged a gentleman of Indian descent adorned in the usual trappings of great affluence, gold etc, he walked towards me and enquired in a broad Yorkshire accent, "Is this Bill's Bangers mate?" As it was now under a different guise I was cautious in my response to this query, always exercise caution when being quizzed about previous ventures was my motto, it saved embarrassment later on. "If you're spending money – it is, if you want money it ain't". I replied with a smile. "Oh I want to spend money mate" came the equally smiling reply to my statement. "Then you've certainly come to the right place, squire" I quipped, adding as a joke, "But if you're wanting to do me a deal with one of those three, I'll tell you now I don't do straight swaps".

If you could see the state of my stock you'd see the joke to be one hell of a good one. My prospective punter burst into laughter at this stage and then asked if he could have a word in the office. I carried on the jovial nature of our meeting, by saying that deals made in the office would be subject to a substantial surcharge. We made our way to the office, whilst his fellow drivers, both of Asian appearance, like himself, elected to inspect our vehicles. (Probably wanted to look at some good cars for a change!)

Once sat down the jewellery bedecked Mercedes driver said in his Yorkshire voice, "I've just bought the missus a 944 (Porsche) from Hansons (main agents up the road from us), and they say they'll knock me off £2000 if I've got a part exchange. So what have you got for about £100". "Nothing mate" was the answer. If he thought he was going to use me to save himself £1900 he was having himself on. Upon hearing my response he pointed to an old Escort on 'death row' which had £100 on the screen, "well what about that one" he enquired. "Ah well I was just about to raise the price of that and all the other cars on here when you came". Especially as he had told me of the generous allowance Hansons were going to give him against one of my cars. "Oh no you can't do that". He said in protest. "I'll go somewhere else then" was his next protest. "Look mate where are you from?" I enquired. "I've come down from Leeds today, why do you ask?" "Well squire I didn't come here on the last banana boat, so lets cut the crap and save us both a lot of time and trouble, you'll be looking all day to find a place to suit you, and I don't think a guy like you can afford to spend all day doing that". I used my most charming voice to good effect, because he then said with a smile, "O.K. We both know the score, if I give you £250 for that Escort will you deliver it up the road for me?" "With pleasure Sir". I pronounced in as pleasant a voice as you like. The Asian Yorkshireman, then pulled out his cheque book. This prompted me to say, "Hold on a minute mate, I only deal in cash, and as nice a fellow as you are I can't accept a cheque from you, I'm afraid no cash no car". He looked at me with great surprise – he probably hadn't used cash to pay for anything in a long while. "I've not got that sort of cash on me". Still trying to keep the mood jovial I said, "Oh yes, they all say that, just before they bounce a cheque on me". His laughing started again, "Look I've just paid for a Porsche on my Gold American Express card, I'm hardly likely to bounce a cheque for £250 now am I?" "They all say something like that as well". I uttered. He then produced his wallet and took out the card in question. I looked as impressed as a vegetarian eyeing up a rump steak. Seeing that I was not swayed, he then produced a £50 cheque guarantee card. I said, "fine, but in that case I want five separate cheques, not in consecutive order, and all with a different date on them please". His face altered slightly, and then returned to his normal smile as he realised why I had requested such a weird arrangement for payment of the agreed sum of £250.

The truth of the matter is this. Banks only have to honour one cheque per day on each £50 guarantee card. They can if they wish (which I have found to be the case more often than not), refuse to cash any subsequent cheques with the number of the guarantee card written on the back, which carry the same date or indeed even a consecutive cheque number. Hence my unusual request. It would take five days for us to get our money, but we were at least getting paid £150 extra for our trouble. The convoy left as quickly as it had arrived, and the Escort was duly delivered. The car was not even a runner, but we didn't mind towing it – after all it was worth £2000 wasn't it? (The most expensive old wreck I had ever delivered.) I can say with hand on heart, that we were never again to have £250,000 worth of cars pull up and buy an old wreck, that was incapable of running, every day of the week.

Carl's wife, Melanie, had an aunt, a woman of large stature who wanted the rest of the world to know, that she was the greatest thing since sliced bread. She would never be 'conned' into buying a wreck, as, according to her that is, she was far too clever for that.

Now to quote a phrase, this was like, 'a red rag to a bull' to yours truly, (I made up my mind to make her eat her words.) Upon asking the name of my intended adversary, Carl told me her surname was none other than, 'Royal'. To the more observant of you, I had cause to sell an Escort some years previously to none other than Mrs Royal. I enquired further and Carl in fact remembered the car in question. I had therefore already made our Mrs Royal eat her words once. I decided to serve her a second course, in one form or another. (I simply loathe the sort of big-mouthed cow, she obviously was.) At this particular time the 'genteel' Mrs Royal had no knowledge of my connection with her nephew-in-law. There was certainly no love lost between Carl and his over-bearing in-law. Although Carl lacked the courage to stand up to her, he had no qualms about me reeking vengeance on his behalf.

As part of her display of her 'influence' over everybody in the family, (in truth the rest of the family were scared rigid by her over-bearing manner, and so tended to do as she directed them to), and hoping to increase her standing (or so she thought), in the local community, she advised a car-seeking neighbour to select a car from her family's garage. (Well, in her eyes it belonged to the family.) She assured her neighbour that she would make sure that they got a very good car, as the rest of the family always did as she asked. Such was the arrogance of our Mrs Royal. Carl did not argue with her demands, he assured me that this was more for his wife's sake than for his own, as he insisted that he was not frightened of the evil cow. He knew however that <u>I ruled the roost</u> at Carl's Cars, and that he had no influence over the running of the place.

The said neighbour was sold an Austin Maestro very cheaply as it turned out. The reason for this being that the car, was 'hit-listed' and not because of any influence from the over arrogant Mrs Royal, besides, I never informed them of the fact, and so they were overjoyed at the bargain they found themselves driving home. 'Hit-listed' is a slang term used throughout the trade, for what quite simply is an accident damaged, and repaired vehicle. All insurance 'write offs' as they are termed must be registered on the central computer at D.V.L.C. Swansea. Any motor dealer selling a 'hit-listed' repaired car, should also disclose the fact that it is indeed such a vehicle, upon selling the car to a member of the general public. I used to get around this by telling half the truth, thereby creating a 'grey area' if ever the sale was to result in a court case. Whenever a punter usually found out a car I had sold was 'hit-listed', and came back *screaming* I managed to wangle out of any problem by reminding them of my disclosure at the time of their purchase, and usually most would not even be bothered as long as the car gave good service and was roadworthy. Incidentally, no court proceedings were ever successfully brought against yours truly or my 'employers'. The easy way to sell a 'Hit-listed' car was like so: during my sales pitch I would quickly drop out that we had 'put a wing on' or 'bolted on a new door' whilst pointing out that no one could tell, and this was the reason it was such a 'bargain' simply because we had done this or that bit of a repair.

Our 'hit-listed', repaired cars, were usually some half the price of our competitors, who were of course selling straight cars. So it went without saying that anyone would have been daft to pay full price, when they could buy one looking equally as nice for half the sum from us. They bit like sharks. After all, the only people who knew that their car had seen bodywork repairs, were us and themselves. They could, and most of them did, pass off their new acquisition as, 'The bargain of the century'.

The man in the street, would not be able to distinguish between one of our cars and one purchased from our fellow motor dealers, apart from the price that is.

Mrs Royal's neighbour was duly relieved of the necessary, (cash), and sent on his way happy as a pig in muck. I am not quite sure what it was that inflamed the pompous Royal woman's rage, it might have been the price that he had paid for such a nice looking car, (creating within her a jealous streak, as her own car had cost her a damn sight more, and was the same age), or the fact that upon looking at the receipt she discovered a vaguely familiar signature, – mine.

She did not dare confront me personally, as it would have been made public, that she had been duped some years earlier, by yours truly, thereby tarnishing her 'reputation'.

She made up her mind there and then to bring about my dismissal, from what she believed to be, the family firm. (Silly cow). When she confronted Carl concerning the matter, all her hopes of sacking me were dashed at a stroke. He informed his dictatorial aunt-in-law, that if I was to be dismissed, the whole place would close down, – end of story.

Maybe the fact that I had 'pulled one over' on her previously, made her over critical about the Maestro. I think her rage fuelled mainly by the price, in comparison to her own car, rather than her fury because it was me who had sold it. Her imagination was in overdrive over the deal, even advising the now bewildered neighbour, to have an independent report on the car, carried out by another garage. (Why had she advised them to go to Carl's place, and assuring them of a good deal, which they subsequently got, if she was now telling them to have it checked by another garage? What must they now be thinking?)

All the 'hit-listed' cars we subsequently sold had a full year's M.O.T. on them, and so there was no question of any of them being unsafe.

The independent report revealed that it was indeed roadworthy but because of evidence of repairs being carried out at sometime in it's history they checked whether or not the car was on the Register. (As would any motor dealer, not just to check for a car being a write off, but also to reveal if any finance, was still owing on any particular vehicle. The check showed clear as regards any outstanding finance, but registered the car as an insurance write-off. This was the only detrimental item found in the report. The neighbour was quite satisfied, that the car was O.K., after all he couldn't really complain about it's registration as a write off, as I had indicated that it had been involved in a collision when he bought it. (We were in the clear because of this disclosure, even though I was a little vague as to the full extent of the original damage.) Mrs Royal however, still inflamed at the cheap price that they had paid, was still not happy with the situation, even though her neighbour was. (Anyone would think that by her behaviour, <u>she</u> had bought the car.) She saw fit therefore, to worry the by now <u>very</u> bewildered, neighbour, to death over the vehicle. She proceeded to declare the car a death trap, and advised in no uncertain terms to get rid of the 'wreck' quick sharp, before it killed them. (Once they had got rid of the car she would have had no reason to be jealous would she?)

After hearing of Mrs Royal's pathetic antics, I thought it about time that I intervened in the matter. I don't know whether it was intuition, good luck, or what, but I had the feeling that our Mrs Royal was hiding something. I took the registration number of her car and ran a check on it. The resultant information was to say the least, very interesting. Not only did she owe a lot of money on the car, (she had told everyone she had bought it for cash), but amazingly, <u>her</u> car was also recorded as a write-off. I couldn't believe my luck.

Her neighbour had paid cash for the Maestro. I rang him and asked if he would call to see me, as I had certain information which he might find very interesting. When he eventually left our meeting he was suitably armed, and the information that I gave him, the perfect ammunition to end the whole affair. Mrs Royal never again raised the subject of the Maestro to Carl. She sold her car a week after my meeting with her neighbour, I wonder why? The Maestro is still serving it's owner well, and has not, to my knowledge, ever let him down. Mrs Royal's replacement car, which incidentally cost her an arm and a leg, and also some two years younger, has had numerous breakdowns. Poetic justice would you say?

I now wish to illuminate the fact that not all the villains in the car sales system are to be found on the side of the dealer, on the contrary, there are all too many unscrupulous characters out there who think, that the sellers of second hand cars to be fair game. If a dealer cons a punter, then he is painted as black as the ace of spades, where as if the punter cons the dealer, this is looked upon as somewhat of an heroic deed. I have lost count of the number of people for instance who were to try and purchase a car with a bouncing cheque. The unsuspecting private man, obviously not as experienced in coping with such con artists, is still all too often the victim of such deception. It is a very rare occasion, if a dealer is found to have been stupid enough to be duped by the likes of these type of people.

Appearance is no indication as to the financial standing of a prospective buyer. I, in fact have sometimes found the opposite to be the case. Just suppose that you were to put yourself in the position of an intended cheque bouncer, what sort of impression would you want to convey to your prospective victim?

Exactly, if you dress and act as if you are of sound financial status, then the odds are more in favour of the victim presuming that the cheque you offer him in payment is worth the money you indeed make it out for. There are those amongst you, that might say that the public is now a lot more wary of cheque fraud. An even cursory glance at the ever growing crime statistics, would soon alter your opinions on that score.

Then of course there is the guy who does have money, but is temporarily out of funds. (Awaiting for his salary to become due for instance.) Because of this impending state of affairs, they are tempted to look for a car, in the hope that by the time the cheque is either presented, or cleared, the money should be in their account. This type of punter is more prevalent than you would first think. The prospect of owning any particular car, rather than missing it, seems to outweigh the risk of the cheque not clearing. Such is the lack of responsibility amongst the impulsive members of our society. The type of car that they will prey upon is usually the bargain that is not to be missed. In this type of circumstance, as I have already said, the gamble is taken to avoid losing the car to another (more than likely cash), equally eager purchaser. Then of course there is the punter who is in need of a car urgently, but finds himself awaiting the arrival of funds, the risk that a cheque may bounce is an easy form of loan, all presuming that the cavalry (cash) arrives on time.

This brings me to an event, which highlights the instance of bouncing cheques, which occurred during one of my very rare bouts of absence from the pitch. I was in the process of viewing five or six bangers, which were being offered for sale by another dealer at the time, which resulted in an absence of forty-five minutes duration. I had left instructions that if at all possible, any prospective punters were to be delayed until my return. Carl however thought this an ideal opportunity, once I had gone, to show me what he had learned of dealing on the pitch.

As it turned out I had not been gone ten minutes, when a school teacher and his wife were to stroll onto the yard. The teacher in question, it turned out, lived in Sheffield, a distance of ten miles away and he needed a car urgently. He had secured a teaching post in Mexborough. This meant apparently, that he found himself in work again after a long period of unemployment. Carl, who was no great academic, and like most people held the teaching profession in some esteem, was taken in by the all too plausible, 'gentleman'.

The educated fraudster, for this was what he was, whether he was a teacher or indeed even if he were a member of the aristocracy, selected a Mk5 Cortina priced at £395 as his intended conveyance to Mexborough on a daily basis.

Carl's ego must have been doing overtime with the thought of being able to impress me on my return with news of his first sale. Despite my warnings about the acceptance of cheques for cars, when the middle-class academic proffered a cheque for the Cortina, Carl accepted it without question. (Obviously thinking that, because he produced I.D. and a National Union of Teachers membership card as proof of who he was, and his assurance that he was not the type to write out dud cheques.) Upon my return he was all aglow as he announced that he had achieved his first sale. My first impression was of admiration, but it soon turned to disappointment once the cheque was produced. "He didn't have enough cash on him, so I had to take a cheque, and before you say anything, it was definitely his cheque book because I asked for I.D., and anyway it won't bounce 'cos he's a teacher". Came the proud statement from Carl. I enquired, "why didn't you ask him to leave a deposit and then send him to the bank for the rest of the cash?". "He said that he needed the car in a hurry,

(I bet he did) and that by the time he got to the bank it would be closed. It's alright it won't bounce he's a teacher". Came the pathetic reply. It was pointless asking any more questions, the bird had flown, there was nothing else to be done until the cheque bounced. Which it would if my experiences were anything to go by. Throughout my years in the car trade I have learned the folly of accepting cheques as payment for cars, and letting the car go before the cheque had cleared. The lecture I felt was necessary was too late to give, and so I never bothered. I would have been only too happy to have been proved wrong on this occasion, but I knew in my heart of hearts that the cheque had an odds on chance of coming back franked by the bank with the words, 'please represent' or 'refer to drawer' both of which meant the same thing.

You could be excused, for thinking that the passing of dud cheques is a rare occurrence, but whilst trading both, Bill's Bangers and Carl's Cars, we were to see such an attempt, on average six times per week. Even as a 'private man' I was to get one or two attempts per car, and so the problem may be a little worse than you think. Not all people are as streetwise as yours truly, so Lord help the innocent private seller.

Sure enough the infamous cheque was returned. The address the teacher gave was the correct one, thanks for small mercies, and a call to directory enquiries produced a telephone number for the cheque-bouncing academic. I dialled the number, and was to hear only one sound, the number unobtainable tone. He had obviously not even paid his phone bill. (Or maybe he had given them a bouncing cheque in payment as well as us.)

It was coincidence that I had to go to Sheffield that day. (To collect a set of trade plates for the newly formed Carl's Cars.) I therefore decided to locate the address the teacher had given to the all too gullible Carl, the week before. Upon finding the address I discovered (surprise, surprise), that no one was at home, or more likely, they were too afraid to answer the door. As luck would have it the Cortina was parked at the rear of the house, I presumed that the teacher must have been hiding in the house. To prevent the removal of the car, to anywhere else, I managed to open the bonnet and remove the rotor arm from the distributor. I then made my way back to the pitch, and fished Bill from out of his workshop. I told him to bring sufficient tools to remove the steering lock from the immobilised Cortina, thus enabling us to drive the car back to the pitch.

It is common knowledge that early Fords have only a small number of variations to their keys. (Well it is common enough knowledge in the trade anyway.) I therefore collected every Ford key that we had on the place, in the hope that one might fit, thus saving removal of the whole ignition. Again luck was to be on our side as the keys I had took were to supply the required result. Within an hour of it's discovery, the Cortina was back in it's rightful place, complete with newly cut keys, on my front line.

The following day I received a phone call, it was from our elusive cheque fraudster, assuring me that if I were to let him take the car, he would pay me the cash – the next day.

It's a marvellous thing, how dishonesty knows no educational or class barriers. Crime it seems to me, is one of society's classless pursuits, it's comforting to know that you can't trust anyone, isn't it? Working class, middle class, or upper class, when it comes to money.

Needless to say the Cortina-less teacher, felt no compulsion to press his request any further, probably due to the fact that I offered him a free vasectomy, if ever he showed his face near my pitch again. I wonder who was to be his next victim, I doubt very much if his rubber cheque crusade would end with us.

CONCLUSION

Despite the efforts of the powers-that-be, I continued to wreak vengeance on behalf of the motor trade, on Joe Public. It was some six months after the council's spotty-faced representatives came to call, that I finally decided to call it a day. Not due to outside pressure, but I suppose you could say the lack of it, was to contribute to the end of Carl's Cars.

We found ourselves in the grip of a recession, the likes of which the motor trade had not seen in a very long while. Just like any other industry, the motor industry was subject to fluctuations in the state of the nation's economy. I have always been of the opinion, that the secondhand car market is a vivid indicator of the financial status of the man in the street. In short, if money was in short supply people tended to display the fact, by their reluctance to spend it. The car trade along with housing market, have long been the financial barometer in the money market. After all is said and done, the general public's greatest financial commitments were largely due to one or the other – or both.

As I have stated throughout this book, money was always of secondary importance in any of my dealings. By far the greater 'turn on', to me was the act of 'pulling off a deal', the more the merrier. Although, in spite of the recession, we were still getting punters, they were only a fraction of the usual. I could have carried on trading I suppose – we were making just enough to get by. But when money is in short supply, those punters that <u>did</u> have it to spend, were very reluctant to part with it. This led to the inevitable – the ratio of 'spyers' to 'buyers' increased dramatically, and there is nothing more certain to dampen a *shearer's* ardour than a distinct lack of *sheep* to shear. I decided, then to, 'throw in the towel'. Once the fun had disappeared I had no incentive to carry on.

If the local council only knew of my philosophy, they may have been able to close us down sooner than we did, but as their efforts only used to inflame my temper, thus creating a challenge to yours truly, by so doing made it fun to 'play' with them. I continued robbing the public for a lot longer than I probably would have, had they not been so eager to achieve my downfall. Ironic really, they tried so hard to close me down, for the sake of the poor public, subsequently failing at every attempt. It was the public themselves in the end, that were to finish me. (Or should I say lack of them?)

Since 'retiring' I have had numerous offers from fellow members of the car trade. I have turned down all their offers of employment, for three main reasons. The first and I suppose most relevant reason was, that after some thirty odd years of *shearing* I was getting tired of the pursuit. Maybe it was my conscience playing on me at last. (That last remark you can believe or not, but I fool myself into thinking it might be true.) The second reason is that I cannot 'work' for anyone else, I would feel too much under pressure to perform, after all said and done, I only did it for the fun. Once you started to work to live, as opposed to living to work, then funnily enough this was my cue to leave. The third and probably the least important, was the fact that there was not enough trade out there, to warrant the efforts of myself. I didn't carry a magic wand (although to the majority of outsiders it may have looked that way.) The world's best salesman can't sell if there is no one to buy. Or in the words of my mate Larry, "You can't get feathers off of a frog."

These then were my premier reasons for me retiring. There is a very remote chance of me coming out of retirement, but all three of the original reasons, must be eradicated first, before I would even give it a fleeting thought. The general public is, therefore safe in the knowledge that I am no longer practising. my noble art.

However, there are a lot of people out there, of similar ability, I'm afraid it will be a very good piece of legislation, that manages to thwart their efforts at *shearing sheep*.

To relate every interesting event, to you the reader, that was to take place at both, Bill's Bangers and Carl's Cars would fill enough volumes to compete with Encyclopedia Brittanica, (And more to the point would fill a few prison cells in the process.) I shall take this opportunity, to reward your patience, (and good taste) in reading this book, with what I believe to be sound advice on the pit-falls of secondhand car purchase.

By far the greatest advice I can give is in two parts, firstly buy the most expensive you can afford. Don't plump for the seemingly obvious bargain. No matter what the price of your prospective purchase, <u>always</u> take a knowledgeable friend along with you. A common fault of the unwary punter is to buy because of pressure from the vendor. Whether it be obvious or more subtly administered, from an over-zealous salesman, or a private man. Any choice you make must be <u>your</u> decision not one made for you by a cunning vendor. It's your money when all is said and done, let's face it you didn't get it from a money tree. (If you did send me a cutting!) The cash probably took you a fair while to accumulate, so it goes without saying, that you would be a fool to part with it in a blazing hurry. By this I mean don't buy the first car that, 'seems' to fit the bill, or be pressured into buying a car by <u>anyone</u>.

If you miss a bargain, so what? There are plenty more out there. Like a lot of things today, you get what you pay for, in general that is, secondhand cars (new ones as well for that matter) are no exception. The 'bargain of a lifetime' could turn out to be a millstone around your neck.

There are bargains to be found, but don't be fooled into thinking the job of finding one is easy. Although salesmen and private vendors alike may tell you otherwise – naturally they have a vested interest don't they? If you can afford to, always buy with cash. (As opposed to getting a car on finance.) When you are 'holding folding' you'd be surprised what doors this will open. Both private vendors and dealers, will nearly always 'haggle' over the price of a car when they see the readies. My advice in this respect is, don't be coy – knock them down, you won't gain anything if you don't try. Even if you only succeed in saving yourself a few pounds, that few quid is better in your pocket than in theirs. I always made a point of 'knocking them down' if anyone refused to haggle, I used to walk away. There were always plenty more out there prepared to negotiate. In my opinion most vendors expect to be offered less, so why disappoint them? Throughout the car trade I have found no price to be firm, there was always room for negotiation, no matter how small the saving, I would never pay the asking price. This was one of the fundamental differences between the *sheep* and the *shearers*. *Sheep* more often than not always paid the asking price, where as the exact opposite was true of the *shearer*.

If you have no mechanical knowledge take someone who has, even if the car you hope to buy is from a friend, in fact, especially if you are buying from a friend. If the car turns out to be a bad one then at least you won't feel obligated to purchase it and friendship should remain intact. Quite the opposite could become true if you indeed bought a bad car from a friend. Would you buy a house without making sure it was not about to fall down around your ears? Exactly, well I certainly wouldn't. Admittedly even a mechanic is no match for a competent *shearer* every time, but the art of sensible car purchase is to reduce the odds against being stung. By far the easiest way of achieving this is to have some form of assurance that your prospective purchase is not going to cost 'a king's ransom' to keep on the road.

Believe it or not, just because the vendor says his is a good car, it doesn't mean he's right. (There are a lot of fibbers out there you know?) If you can employ the services of a good mechanic, by far the best place to purchase a car is from one of the numerous car auctions up and down the country. Dependent upon the amount of money you are willing (or indeed are able) to spend, there are a lot of bargains to be had. Here again the 'get what you pay for' rule may be applied, although this is not strictly true in the case of some types of auction.

As a private purchaser at car auctions you have an advantage in that you are buying a car for your own use, not to resell for a profit. (Presumably.) This means that any likely bargain could be snatched from the hands of a hopeful dealer, for obvious reasons. For example, lets suppose that the car you have set your heart on is for sale in the classifieds section of your local newspaper, or at a dealers – the asking price is £2000. At auction the same car should realise around, (pure guesswork based upon experience), £1100 – £1300, dependent upon the bidding. Presuming that your mechanic gives it the O.K. this creates a saving of at least £700. I can hear you saying, "But what if the car breaks down, at least from a dealer you can take it back and have it repaired." With £700 in your pocket, and presuming that your mechanic has done his job correctly, there is no need for the 'security of buying from a dealer'. Anyway all the dealers I have known would be very reluctant to do repairs after the statutory twenty-eight days that they are liable for repairs has elapsed. The problems you may be likely to come across would not warrant the whole of the £700 saving to be spent in rectification. There are a few reasons for buying from an auction besides the possible savings. The main one being, that there is no pressure put upon you to buy. I think it a very good experience for the prospective purchaser of a car to visit an auction anyway, as I can assure you, it would prove most educational. You might also have the opportunity to see first hand, the profit that dealers find it possible to make.

After many years in the motor trade, I would like to think that I had learned a trick or two during that time. But the car trade like so many others, is changing every day. Just when you think there could be an easier way of pulling off a certain thing, up pops a fresh idea and bites you on the backside. What took me years to learn, most of it came with ease, I hope I have passed a little onto you. (Well there are a number of tricks that I dare not disclose in print, for fear of gaining a free holiday.) Even if all this book does is to amuse you, at least I shall not have wasted my time, nor importantly yours. Some of you reading this, oh sorry all of you, will think me to be one of life's villains, you would be quite right to think so. I tend to fool myself into believing that at least I am now an ex-villain, (because if it were not true I would not dare write this book), in the eyes of the philosophers amongst you, I am probably seeking salvation for my past sins. I could be trying to achieve by exposing the inner most secrets of the car trade. Who am I trying to Kid? I must therefore end this attempted book, by giving you a final piece of advice, by the use of two words, which sum up the whole approach to car buying (new or old) today, they are:

BUYER BEWARE!